WHEN THE CHERRY BLOSSOMS FALL

My Life In Japan

By Kim M Hotzon

This book is dedicated to my beautiful daughters,
Breanne and McKenna and to my husband, Bill,
who shared this incredible journey with me.

TABLE OF CONTENTS

FOREWORD

One early evening, when I was two years old, my mother discovered that I was missing from my crib. She searched the house for me, having no clue as to my whereabouts. Somehow, I had managed to climb out of my crib and wander outside. I was found across the street, standing quietly under the glow of a streetlight. Six months later, I was hauling my little push car up and down a nearby road, screeching with pure joy as my little ducky propelled me down the center line. You could say that my desire to travel began then, but it definitely kicked into high gear when I turned five. I remember watching "Chitty-Chitty-Bang-Bang" for the first time. I was enthralled by the adventures of the children as they flew over the land in their little car, exploring picturesque valleys and beaches before finally arriving at a majestic palace in the mountains. Oh, how I fantasized about visiting that sweet factory so I could twirl a whistling striped candy in my mouth! How wonderful it would be to live in a rambling old house and have my breakfast tumble onto my plate off of a conveyor belt! I soon began to dream about travelling the world, and I felt an indescribable need to discover what else may be out there. The world was a fascinating place and my child's mind soaked up every little detail. I would spend hours playing outside, building cities out of leaves and branches, or clearing paths through the bush, stopping to watch snakes or frogs as they scrambled for safety behind trees or under rocks. There were endless summer days at the beach where I collected driftwood and seaweed, or built sandcastles before the tide came in and washed it all away. I was curious about the world around me and I knew that someday I would see it beyond the street I lived on. Growing up in Vancouver, B.C., I had a safe and comfortable way of life but my mind expanded like a jellyfish out of water when I visited Mexico as an adolescent and saw a different part of the world for the first time. I was amazed by the palm trees and vibrant music, and by the pelicans following us into restaurants. I would gather seashells and swim alongside the fish, while crabs and turtles scuttled and slithered on the sand. My skin would turn golden brown as I munched on salsa and freshly caught prawns, feeling the warmth of the salty wind on my body. As a result of those trips, I continued to crave travelling and by the age of 22 that desire would bring me halfway across the world to Japan; a journey which would have a profound effect on me and which would alter the course of my life.

Japan was and continues to be a land of contradictions, merging ancient and dynastic customs with the fast-paced, technological modern world. When my fiancé Bill and I first arrived in Japan, we visited Kyoto's *Kinkaku-ji* temple, otherwise known as the Golden Temple. In the gardens, we stood gazing at the temple, marvelling at the brilliance of the light dancing off of the gold foil encasing the temple. The setting was idyllic, the temple perched regally on a tiny island in the middle of a small lake. Throngs of people passed around us and stopped to look briefly at the fish swimming in the water. Bill and I remained where we stood, for quite some time, mesmerized by such a breathtaking view. The fish were swimming wildly, bumping into each other, frantically looking for food as it was tossed into the water by the tourists. The setting was so peaceful and yet the pond, like the gardens, was crowded. I suddenly felt like the fish, penned in and swimming in every direction looking for an escape route. It would take me 2 years and many life changing experiences before I could stand here again at this pond and truly enjoy the moment.

Japan was to be an adventure for us and like all adventures there were ups and downs, scary moments and wonderful memories to cherish. When we chose to leave Canada, we sold everything we owned and quit our jobs, mine as a receptionist at a Vancouver real estate company and Bill's as a supervisor for Save-On Foods. We set out to teach English in a foreign country with only our passports and our eagerness. We had zero knowledge of the Japanese language, we lacked sponsorship and we had, literally, only a few dollars in our pockets. We anticipated that we would earn good money teaching English while being able to travel around Asia and make friends along the way. What we didn't anticipate were weeks of living in segregated youth hostels, serious health problems and extreme culture shock. There were times when we struggled to afford meals or winter clothing.

During the 2 years that we lived there, we became quite acclimatized to Japanese culture and we developed meaningful friendships. In writing my story, I hope to share the magic of this country and its people but also the challenges of trying to fit into a society that may not always feel welcome to outsiders. Though my story is at times dramatic, and I am sure not everyone travelling to Japan to live there will experience all that I did, I do hope readers will gain some sense of the Japanese culture through this book for Japan is a very unique country in Asia.

Our life in this country, with its rich symbolism rooted in history, happened during the early nineties. While many aspects of the Japanese culture will have changed since then, many others will have remained exactly as they were when we were living there. Living in Japan changed my life forever and it was also the beginning of a lifelong career in the field of education. I am grateful for the experience and even for the challenges I faced as it strengthened my character and helped to shape who I am today. Like the cherry blossoms, my life in Japan was momentous; an incomparable and beautiful moment in my life. It was also short lived, abruptly ending, leaving just a trace of my existence behind. I will always feel emotionally connected to Japan. It remains a country full of paradoxes yet it will always be a culture to be admired.

Kim Hotzon

Vancouver, March 2012

CHAPTER 1

The Other Side of the World

I was sitting on the balcony of my apartment when the lightning hit. The deafening rumble of the thunder came first and before I could react and run inside to safety, the fork of light came down, splitting the sky open with its crooked, menacing fingers. I watched transfixed as it hit the satellite dish on the building across from me. Then I heard the wind as it picked up and slammed against the side of the building. With my hair whirling around my head and blocking my vision, I stumbled over the lawn chair, hearing it fly against the railing of concrete. This was a fierce storm. The kind of storm that rarely happens in the city of Vancouver. Still holding onto my wineglass, I flew inside and slammed the sliding door shut. I changed into dry clothes and poured another glass of wine. I looked out at the wind and rain pelting the window and wondered where my boyfriend was. He was usually home before me as I worked in the city at a real estate office and my drive home each day was longer than his. I typically came home to find dinner cooked and waiting for me. As I reached for the phone, I heard the front door slam shut and Bill came striding in.

Bill walked over to the sliding door and opened it up. "Unbelievable storm eh?" he asked.

"No! Leave it shut, the rain is coming inside," I said. I was more frightened of the lightning but it was also cold and wet outside.

"How was your day? Lots of traffic?" he asked as he peeled off his shoes and sat down beside me.

I poured a glass of wine and handed it to him, wincing as the lightning struck again. "Nah, it was a pretty good drive today, no accidents at least. Where were you at?"

"Looking at fishing gear. I need a new reel," he answered, as he leaned back into the couch.

1

Ah, yes, trout fishing was around the corner. I thought about my dad who loved to fish and how he wouldn't be up here much anymore to go fishing. It was 1989 and I was a young woman stuck in a 9 to 5 job, without any real focus or purpose. Most of my family members were living far away, immigrating to the United States while I remained behind. I missed them terribly but I was now on my own, trying to make my way. But I had a dream folded up inside my brain, silently tucked away. I wanted to see the world and this dream would soon become a reality but it would unfold unlike anything I could have imagined. I was working as a receptionist to bring in money and my life seemed to be going nowhere. At 22 years of age I did not consider myself overly ambitious but I knew I wanted to do more with my life. I was held back from my goals just trying to survive. Life moved along, but without family or a meaningful job within my grip, I felt lonely and dissatisfied. I had been tossing around the idea of spending a few months in Virginia with my family to be near them again and to immerse myself in a new environment where maybe I might figure out what I wanted to do with my life. Bill, unsurprisingly, did not react well to this idea of mine. Though I considered our relationship to be a good one, I was definitely not ready for marriage or children just yet and I was eager to forge my path in life. Despite the fact that we had only shared a couple of discussions regarding my desire to get away and see the world, it seemed that Bill was feeling just as unanchored as I was. We were both adventurers by nature, excited by new people and places.

Bill leaned over and clasped my hand as I forced myself to look away from the window, feeling the fear creep up. I was deathly afraid of thunder and lightning storms, believing they could snake in under the cracks of the doors and windows and kill every living thing in their path.

"Hey, I was thinking about........well, maybe we should try something different, maybe move away and get new jobs.........in Japan," Bill said suddenly.

For my boyfriend of 2 years to spontaneously suggest an overseas trip when money was tight seemed a funny choice to make.

"*What?*" I laughed. "Why Japan?"

The idea was so out of left field that I found it bizarre. I waited for him to give me some kind of explanation.

"We could teach English," he answered casually, almost as if he were talking about what we should have for dinner. There was no weight in his words, yet I could tell that he wasn't joking about this.

"Right. Uh, so I'm not happy with my life, and you think we should fly around the world and *teach English*....in *Japan*?" I was quiet for several moments trying to make sense out of this conversation. I drank the rest of my wine while looking at him and mulling his words over.

"We could go there and teach English as a job. We could make money and survive that way. It would give us a chance to travel and get away from Vancouver," he responded. He seemed to have really thought this over.

I still wasn't certain if he was being serious, or just idly talking. Finally I asked him "Do you mean that you would give up your job and leave everything, just like that, and take off?"

"Why not?" Bill replied. He leaned over and grinned at me as he gave me a hug. "You're not happy here with your job and neither am I. So why not? The thing is Kim, we *can*."

Glancing out the window, I suddenly realized that the wind had died down, and the thunder and lightning had stopped. What a weird night.

When I realized that Bill was actually considering living in Japan, we then began an earnest discussion of how we might accomplish this. We realized that without children or flourishing careers there was little keeping us tied to Vancouver. I believe that this was the moment when I first understood how life can present you with unexpected opportunities. It was an incredible, yet scary feeling, to think that we could actually sell everything and just *go*. We talked long into the night and when I awoke the next morning I felt different in a light, unrestrained way. I had a reason now to be excited about life and I had something to look forward to beyond commuting to a clerical job which gave me no satisfaction.

Several weeks passed before we made a conscious decision to actually commit ourselves to this plan. Once we had decided that yes, we were going to do this, it became clear that there were a lot of loose ends to tie up and things to be done before we could leave. Bill and I began advertising our vehicles and furniture and we gave notice at our jobs. The next task was to notify our friends and families of our crazy plan. I remember this time well and the feeling that there was no turning back. People were excited for us and supported our idea of undertaking this once in a lifetime opportunity. We talked to as many people as we could who knew something about Japan and we searched for books on teaching English overseas. At the time, there was little information available about the realities of living and working in Japan. I also had a couple of business suits made for me by a girlfriend and we went out and bought luggage and extra bottles of shampoo and toothpaste. In an era shortly before the explosion of the internet, we did not know if such basic supplies would be hard to find over there. How little we knew! We booked our tickets at a travel agency in downtown Vancouver and closed our bank accounts. The spring passed by quickly and summer arrived. We floated through the remaining weeks blind to the mundane routines surrounding everyone else.

The beginning of our journey, Vancouver International *Airport, August 1989*

4

On the day of departure, August 3, 1989, we stood at the check-in counter at the Vancouver International Airport. Both sets of our parents stood nearby and everyone was emotional. We were not just going on a vacation, we were going away, far away, for an indefinite period of time. Our parents shared a quick cup of coffee with us, wishing us well and probably trying to look happy for us while secretly wondering if we would be okay. It had been a surreal atmosphere and a few people were looking our way as tears flowed and the excitement in our voices boomed throughout the room. For our part, Bill and I were excited to be leaving. After passing through security, we found our seats in the waiting area at our departure gate. Sitting down on the plastic chairs, I could feel my heart racing with excitement, while at the same time, I had a funny, gnawing feeling in my gut as to what we would do once we got there. I had always been a person who carefully planned my days, setting goals and knowing where I would be and what I would be doing at any given time. This was not like me and I knew that there would be no one waiting at the Narita airport to greet us, no home to go to, no job, just this open, unknown reality, and it kind of frightened me. We reflected on all we had been through the past few months regarding our decision to leave the country to go teach English. I looked down at my new engagement ring, bought the week before. I had been informed by a realtor at the office where I had worked that western women could be looked down upon if they were unmarried and living with a man, and so we decided to get engaged prior to leaving. We were beginning a new chapter in our lives.

When the agent announced it was time for departure we grabbed our carry-on luggage and headed over to stand in line. I held out my new passport which the agent stamped and we were pointed through the door toward the plane. Bill and I found our seats on the plane and stowed away our carry-on luggage. Already, I felt a new and different vibe to this journey compared to my earlier travel experiences. The flights to Mexico had been on smaller planes and most passengers were families or couples heading on their holidays. I realized that nearly everyone on this plane was male, dressed in a suit, likely heading home after a business trip. We hadn't left the ground yet but I could sense that our lives were going to be quite different from now on. Settling in, my thoughts turned to our destination of Tokyo and I was both nervous and full of anticipation. I looked down at my new navy blue cotton skirt and blazer feeling like I was dressed to impress. I was not yet aware that my clothing would pale in comparison to what the Japanese wore. I thought about how I had always expected to land in Europe with a backpack and a rail pass trekking through historic villages and hilltop hamlets. All I really knew about Japan were images I had seen from movies like *Shogun* and *Gung Ho*. I understood, of course, that Japan was an industrialized, modern nation with large cities, but I didn't know too much about the culture beyond the stereotypical images of kimono clad geishas and the snow capped Mt. Fuji.

I asked the flight attendant for a cup of orange juice while I wistfully dreamt about the Japan I was anxious to see. I closed my eyes and conjured up images of a traditional country the way I imagined it, the way I wanted it to be. I pictured a mountain path, winding steeply through bamboo, dense and quiet, with moisture heavy in the air, and a little wooden bridge crossing a stream. I visualized a woman walking alone, her brilliantly coloured kimono, held fast with an obi sash. I could see her crossing the bridge with tiny steps as her shoes clicked down on the wooden slats. As she approached a small teahouse, she knelt down to remove her shoes. Her raven black hair was pinned into a tight split bun, sitting high up on her head, exposing her delicate neck. Turning, she seemed to see something behind her, before quickly entering the building. I wondered who was in the house with her, was she entertaining clients by singing or pouring sake, or warming her feet by the coals? I sighed, snuggling under my blanket, thinking that Japan must be a beautiful place, while I hoped sleep would ease some of the time of this long flight.

Out of this reverie I awoke to lights turning on, voices around me and the smell of heated tinfoil wafting through the cabin.

I looked over at Bill who was still sound asleep and gently nudged him awake.

"It looks like our meal is coming," I said as I glanced up the aisle, listening to my stomach gurgle. By now I was starving.

"What'll it be? A nice steak, ya think?" Bill laughed. He was worried about the food in Japan, after eating meat his whole life he thought it was going to be sushi from here on in.

We ate our meal of chicken and potatoes feeling satisfied and feeling our excitement creep up again. I looked out the window and was amazed to see islands below. I grabbed Bill's arm. "Look, that must be Hawaii!"

Bill pulled out our map from the airline seat pouch, flipped it open, and pointed to a group of islands that were situated northward. My heart sank.

"Ha! Ha! Those are the Aleutian Islands!" "You're cute," he said as he gave me a hug.

"One day, we'll get to Hawaii too!" I said excitedly. With visions of turquoise blue water and palm trees swaying over the white sand etched in my mind, I imagined both of us surfing on the beaches of Waikiki. I was ready to see the world.

We had by now crossed the international date line and we were into a new day, August 4th, after a 9 hour flight. At some point throughout the flight my ankles and feet had begun to swell and as we neared Narita Airport I began to worry about how I was going to walk off the plane. I had removed my shoes earlier as the swelling had increased so much that my shoes no longer fit. After the plane landed I walked off barefoot into the airport ignoring the many stares I received along the way. The airport staff had our luggage unloaded in no time and just a short time later we entered customs. With a check of our passports we were admitted entry into Tokyo, Japan.

The first impression I had when we left the coolness of the air-conditioned airport was the muggy, diesel fumed air and the incredible noise outside. I searched the area for palm trees and saw none. Hmmm.... I should have looked closer at the pictures in that book

I read, I thought to myself. We boarded an airport shuttle bus and arrived at our hotel in downtown Tokyo. It was dark and after 7:00 p.m. when we arrived at our hotel. Inside we were treated to a beautiful sight. The lobby was very elegant with giant marble columns, floor to ceiling mirrors and expensively upholstered furniture. I was struck by the decadent image, something which I would learn is very important to the Japanese, who strive to improve upon everything, making things into their own idealized version. We would eventually see elaborate examples of this in restaurants, parks and clubs. One nightclub we went to had been built to resemble an enormous Egyptian tomb, complete with giant sized pharaohs guarding the entrance.

Feeling jet-lagged and weary because of the 17 hour time difference we were ready to get some rest. My feet had continued to swell and I was becoming alarmed at their size. I had no idea what was happening but I put it down to heat and exhaustion. I had no idea yet that it was a sign of a serious health problem that would affect my stay in Japan in the near future. I laid down on the bed, thinking that getting off my feet and elevating them would help.

It was about 3:00 a.m. when we awoke and I called room service for some coffee. Shortly afterward the bellboy arrived with a thermos full of coffee for a price of ¥800 (then the equivalent of about US$6.00). Now considering that we were very tight with money this seemed like an indulgence, especially to Bill who did not drink coffee. I learned rather quickly that coffee, among other things, was very expensive!

Our room was situated on the 21st floor overlooking the city of Tokyo. Though the view was incredible I searched earnestly for any sign of greenery. What lay before my eyes was a massive concrete jungle. Tokyo was an unending horizon of gray concrete skyscrapers. I closed the curtains and lay back on the bed beside Bill. His sister Laura was living in Yamato, Yokohama, a two hour train ride from our hotel. We called her up and let her know that we had made it and that we would meet her outside the train station in Yamato. The swelling in my feet had gone down considerably and we decided it was time to go. After leaving the hotel in the morning we began wheeling our four enormous suitcases down the sidewalk in search of the subway. Now, we had not properly thought out the practicality of having so much luggage without a vehicle. It was difficult and embarrassing to be pulling all that luggage such a long way. Walking along the streets I sensed that something was out of place. Finally it struck me what was missing. "Have you noticed there aren't any people, *anywhere*?" I asked him.

Bill only shrugged as he was so intent on getting to where we were going. But I felt uneasy trying to figure it out. I looked at my watch, it was ten minutes to nine. In Vancouver at this time of morning there would be people everywhere walking to work. I kept walking and pulling my suitcases feeling like I was in the middle of a sound stage for Planet of the Apes. Block after block and we encountered no people. Eventually we saw some steps leading down to a subway. Vancouver did not have an underground subway and relied mainly on vehicles and transit buses to ferry people around. Although we were not worldly with mass commuter rail we were totally unprepared for what we encountered upon heading down into the subway. We were jolted into such a shock that I will never forget. As we entered the dark cavernous underground we were assaulted with millions of faces swarming in a mad frenzy in every direction. People were moving so fast that you literally got pushed along with them. I felt suffocated. The Japanese people must have thought we were an apparition, entering a busy subway with 4 suitcases, 2 duffle bags and 2 ski coats bunched under our arms. What a sight we must have been! It was no easy task lugging our belongings in the oppressive humidity for it was very muggy down there. Sweat had begun trickling down our bodies the instant we had left the hotel and we were now drenched.

There were several different levels in the subways and going up and down the stairs was a major undertaking. We would run a suitcase down, pray that it would be there when we came back, head up the stairs again and grab another bag until we had everything together again. After only a few minutes in the subway catastrophe struck when one of the wheels broke on the big suitcase and Bill resorted to dragging the bulk behind him. Bill, being six feet tall, towered above most Japanese people and the image of him with his height and size dragging that broken suitcase across the subway floor with such determination must have appeared strange to many of those morning commuters. Now lost and confused, we searched the sea of faces for any sign of help. We saw a couple of tourists passing by and I ran over waving my arms.

"Excuse me!" I shouted. "Can you help us?"

"We want to go to......Ya-ma-to....in Yokohama, where can we buy tickets?" I asked. The worry and stress must have been visible on our faces.

The man smiled. He initially spoke German but had no trouble switching easily to English for us 'Americans'. "Here, you can have this map of the Tokyo subway system, you'll need it," the man replied. They were evidently in a hurry and so they wished us luck as they walked off down the stairs.

We continued walking along, trying to understand the map and eventually we arrived at the ticket area. Japan uses the same writing system as China. Basically, they use characters known as *kanji* with their own version of characters known as *katakana* and *hiragana* intermixed. For Bill and I it was like trying to read hieroglyphics. The strokes of the characters on every sign merely looked like spaghetti noodles to us. We eventually figured out how to get a ticket from the maze of kanji symbols on the machine and made our way to the platform. We needed to change trains twice and figured it would take two to two and a half hours to arrive in Yamato. I had no idea at that point that in the near future I would be taking these trains on my own, having to find my way to various companies to teach English.

During that train ride we were finally able to see what Japan really looked like. I suppose my expectations were of clean, quaint villages interspersed with lush, green vegetation. The reality was more like tiny homes squished side by side, perched almost on top of the tracks with concrete buildings everywhere the eye could see. In some cases you could see the odd rice field wedged in between a house and an office building.

Tokyo and its surrounding districts are situated on the main island of Japan known as Honshu. It is mostly made up of mountain ranges with a few plains along the coastal areas. Though there are several large cities throughout the island, the main cities are Tokyo to the north and Osaka and Kyoto to the southeast. Hiroshima, the city known around the world for the catastrophic damage it sustained during World War II from the nuclear bomb, sits further southward toward the western side of the island. There is a Peace Memorial Shrine in Hiroshima which houses burnt wreckage and artifacts from the nuclear bomb to remind people of the devastation war brings and to remember its victims. Osaka has a major shipping port along with the neighbouring city of Kobe. It is a heavily populated island. To the north, is the island of Hokkaido and it is widely known in Japan for its ski resorts and natural beauty with its rugged terrain. To the south of Honshu is Kyushu Island, a heavily industrialized region, while furthest south is the island of Okinawa, known to many Americans because of the presence of the American military base. Knowing that Honshu was heavily populated I expected many people but I was unprepared for the denseness of the city. Yet the Japanese have skillfully utilized what available land there is and they have taken advantage of the underground to build mini cities with stores and restaurants.

~

After three and a half hours we finally made it to Yamato. We left the station and crossed the street to McDonald's, a welcome and familiar sight. We planted ourselves down on the edge of the road to wait for Laura. The sweat continued to roll off of our foreheads and with futile attempts we wiped it away as passersby stared at us and our luggage. We had been there about an hour when Laura walked up with tears in her eyes, happy to see familiar faces. She wrapped her arms around Bill and quietly cried while I stood back. It was clear that this was an emotional meeting and that she was in need of some familiar company. She reached out to give me a quick hug.

"It is so good to see you guys. I have to apologize though, as I have been called back to teach this afternoon so you'll have to make your own way to my apartment." Laura said. She turned around to begin the short walk back to her place.

Bill and I just stood there for a moment somewhat taken aback.

"How will we find our way?" I wondered aloud.

"You will have no problem. Just follow me the first two blocks then you will turn left at the corner and my apartment is a block further down," Laura answered. She was in a hurry to get back to work so we gathered our luggage and began walking.

Yamato is a small district and outside of the central part of Tokyo, so foreigners were unusual in this area. Since the other English teachers had left the country, Laura was the only foreigner in the entire town. After she took us the first two blocks and went inside her building to teach class, Bill and I, with our directions, made our way to her apartment to drop off our luggage and then set out to explore the area. I was surprised at some of the similarities between Japan and Mexico, the only other country I had visited. There were the same narrow little streets lined with old stores, merchandise piled upon the sidewalks. There were also neon signs blinking everywhere and most evident were the masses of people. We noticed how many people were staring at us with distinct curiosity. We would soon learn that we were considered *gaijin*, literally translated as 'outsiders'. In Japanese society, although many people are warm and courteous like elsewhere in the world, it is often very hard to break through the inner circle of society and be accepted as one of them. As we walked along the side streets we garnered more attention and so I stared back, thinking how I had expected all Japanese people to be four feet tall and surprised at how many were taller than myself. This was one of several stereotypes I would learn during my life in Japan. One of the biggest stereotypes we found in Japan was the idea that everything would be very expensive. Like all cities, Tokyo had inexpensive and reasonably priced things if you knew where to find them. Some items were indeed priced ridiculously high and it wasn't unusual to see certain fruits like cantaloupe or watermelons, which are imported, priced at US$50.00 each. These fruits, however, were in perfect shape, with not a scratch or bruise on them; the Japanese prided themselves on image and appearance in everything they undertook and they did this well. If you wanted to be more careful with your money you could buy bananas or pineapple which were moderately priced. Clothing was available at a range of prices and if you shopped around you could find deals like anywhere else. It was a challenge to find clothing that fit. The younger generation of Japanese people were much taller but they were still much slimmer and narrower in their builds when compared to North American and European men and women. Though I was considered petite by western standards I would nevertheless find it difficult in the months ahead to find clothing and shoes that fit. Already I was learning about consumerism in Japan.

Later in the afternoon we met Laura for lunch and we were delighted to see western food of different varieties available. We had a chance to relax for awhile and ask Laura how her life had been in the past few months. During our conversation we realized how often she was required to teach and we were not expecting such a demanding schedule.

We watched as Laura deftly picked up her noodles with her chopsticks, something we would have to learn. "I work a long day, from morning until afternoon, then I have a couple of hours of classes in the evening," she explained.

"What days do you get off?" I asked. I felt frustrated as I tried to not look like a 2 year old while eating. Clearly, for me, eating and talking at the same time as learning to use chopsticks was not a good idea.

"The weekends are mine," Laura said. She looked thoughtful and so I asked her what she usually did with her free time.

"I have taken some trips to hot springs and I've been to visit some of my student's homes and I have seen a Kabuki show. Mom and Bob are coming in a couple of months to visit and so I 'm planning to take them to a hot spring village a couple of hours away," she said.

After eating, we went to a nearby shop to buy our futons and a fan which we were told we would definitely need in this hot weather.

With the level of humidity in the summer months and the coldness of the winters it is very difficult to survive comfortably without modern appliances. Apartments, or 'mansions' as the Japanese call them, do not typically come equipped with central heating or air-conditioning, nor do they generally have refrigerators or stoves. It is considered the responsibility of the tenant or owner to acquire the necessary appliances and comforts that we take for granted at home. Even lighting is often not provided and you must buy your own light fixtures. One of the coolest things about Japanese culture, however, is what gaijin referred to as *gomi* hunting, otherwise known as garbage hunting. Because Japanese society revolved around consumerism, and Japanese homes were not large, there was very little storage space and as a result you could find nearly new television sets, furniture, radios, almost anything you might need to set up your apartment, sitting right on the sidewalk. Many foreigners would be walking down a street, spot a table or a television set on the side of the road and haul it back to their apartment.

The Giant Buddha in Kamakura

The next two days brought torrents of rain and we knew we had to start looking for work. Without sponsorship, foreigners could only stay in Japan for a maximum of three months. We travelled to the nearby city of Fujisawa and found a copy of the Japan Times, an English printed newspaper, which we then scoured for any available work near the city. It was disappointing to find no jobs available because Fujisawa was a green city and we felt comfortable there. Despite this unproductive morning, we took advantage of our available time by visiting the nearby Giant Buddha in Hase, Kamakura. We found the train ride scenic as it wound around the coastline with a beautiful hilltop on our left. When we arrived at the station, we had to hike up several stone steps in order to reach the Buddha. The statue was beautiful and the setting was breathtaking. Many decades ago a great tsunami wave washed away the temple that once stood over the Buddha but the Buddha statue survived and remains a symbol of strength, high up on a hill overlooking the Sea of Japan.

~

We spent the rest of the week with Laura but we were disillusioned with the area. We felt that there should be more work opportunities closer to Tokyo and so we left and made our way to the Yoyogi Youth Hostel in Shinjuku District, Tokyo. The youth hostel was run down, with cracks in the walls and worn tile and linoleum covering the floors. It had originally been built for the athletes during the 1968 Olympic Games held in Tokyo. I felt instantly depressed as I had never stayed in such bare surroundings and our money was running low.

During our five days at the youth hostel we intermittently looked for work while visiting local attractions. One afternoon we wandered through the Imperial Palace Gardens which were truly immense. The sun was blisteringly hot and the humidity was strong and we soon became tired from all the walking we were doing. The intensity of the heat was something we had never experienced.

I stopped to catch my breath as I gazed at the rows and rows of manicured lawns and hedges.

"Let's find somewhere to get a drink," I suggested. My mouth was dry and I felt dehydrated as I wiped the sweat from my forehead.

"Good idea," Bill said. He was perspiring heavily as he turned back to walk over to me.

We continued walking down a wide, expansive path surrounded by bonsai trees and other neatly trimmed shrubs. Suddenly, a noise like a thousand sprinklers went off all around us.

"What the heck is that?" I asked.

Bill looked around, upwards and downwards, totally confused. The noise was deafening. He pointed to a nearby tree and said "It sounds like it's coming from the trees."

Stepping closer, we stood at the base of the nearest tree. Clearly, the noise was louder. Slowly, we began to notice large insects that resembled cockroaches with big wings. These insects, called cicadas, were letting off a chirping sound that drowned the air with its incessant buzzing frenzy. We laughed hysterically as we walked closer together, marvelling at such a strange thing.

We were still searching for somewhere to buy a drink as we worked our way through the gardens toward the youth hostel. Walking along the trail, we encountered a group of Shinto shrines, known as *Meiji Jingu*. The buildings were constructed in 1920 following the deaths of the Emperor Meiji, and his consort, Empress Shoken. Although the original buildings were destroyed during the air raids of World War II, they were subsequently rebuilt in the late 1950's. Emperor Meiji was the first modern Emperor of Japan, following centuries of feudal rule. During his reign, Japan underwent significant changes and evolved into a modern country. During the Emperor's lifetime, he and Empress Shoken were known to visit the gardens. The shrines were built in their memory and they housed calligraphy, clothing, artwork and other artifacts of the Emperor and Empress. During our visit we learned that Shinto was the original religion of Japan and although it has no holy book, adherents practice simple values including the connection between nature and harmony. The surrounding gardens were beautiful, with small ponds outlined in irises, the Empress's favourite flower. We stood and watched an elderly man as he painted the landscape on a small easel. It was very peaceful in these surroundings and I tried to imagine what it felt like for the Empress as she would have stood here many decades ago.

As we left the shrine area, we were on the verge of dehydration when we finally spotted a vending machine. We eagerly dropped our money in and grabbed our drinks, guzzling as quickly as we could. We had noticed a strange concept in Japan where beer could be purchased from vending machines on practically every street corner. Imagine this convenience and how it would go down at home in Vancouver, especially on hockey nights! Yet the youth here were seemingly well-behaved without a lot of stumbling, drunken young people around. I wondered at this cultural difference and how our youth would never show such restraint. We were told that beer drinking was discouraged here before a certain age, but when it's out in the open, it seems too accessible. In time, we would discover the problems that are often associated with drinking in Japanese culture.

The next afternoon we were strolling through the Meiji gardens again when we heard a loud commotion sounding like many people screaming in the distance. We stopped in our tracks, both of us thinking that some sort of riot was taking place on the other side of the garden. We hesitated a moment or two but the noise seemed to be staying beyond the tree line so even though we had no idea what was happening, curiosity led us in that direction. We wound our way through the paths and came out onto a wide boulevard. All we could see was a mass of people, some of whom were parading around in spiked purple hair looking like garish versions of Elvis Presley. It was the district's Rock Music Fair, where young people got together in a kind of Woodstock fashion and performed their music free for the masses. Some of the female performers were known as *harajuku* girls, whom Gwen Stefani famously drew inspiration from years later when she incorporated their style into her world tour.

"This is unbelievable!" I shouted. "Look at those girls, they look like Pippi Long Stocking! They look like little girls..........."

17

We were transfixed by the energy and the incredible wall to wall throng of people humming all around us. There were groups of people everywhere, many of them so obviously young, and even though I was only twenty-two years old I felt light years older than they looked and behaved. I would discover during my time in Japan that across the culture, young men and women behaved much more differently than their western counterparts. They seemed to possess less emotional maturity and would giggle and behave more like elementary students when they were nervous or embarrassed. It was something I found fascinating as the age gap between them and myself was only about five years. After spending the afternoon immersed in feudal Japan amid artwork and tranquillity, we were now enveloped in the new Japan, where the youth seemed eager to pursue lifestyles like that of western youth, choosing their own partners and doing what they wanted to do with their life. This existence of contradiction in lifestyles between the older and younger generations became ever more apparent throughout our stay in Japan. Some of the young Japanese people went on televised dating game shows to choose a mate. Many young women found their husbands through their company where they worked and although the majority of young women were still expected to quit working once married, a few were continuing to keep their jobs, breaking with a long-held tradition in a patriarchal society.

It was during our stay at the youth hostel that we responded to a positive looking advertisement in the Japan Times newspaper that was looking to hire English teachers. After calling and scheduling an interview, we made our way to the head office of a small English Language company in Tokyo. However, during the interview it seemed that the teachers were needed to work on Kyushu Island, way down south, an island known mainly for its industry. This did not seem favourable to us and without further consideration we thanked the interviewers for their time, got up and left. It was beginning to become a tense situation as we were now very low on money and yet there seemed to be no decent job opportunities at all.

Later that night, sitting in my segregated room at the youth hostel, I tried to analyze our situation. I knew that I did not like Tokyo because of the crowds and the lack of greenery inside the city and yet we could not afford to keep travelling. We desperately needed to find jobs. As I sat there deep in thought a young blond woman came in and sat down on a bed by the window. I am sure she could sense that I was distracted and worried. She looked over and smiled and with a noticeably Australian accent introduced herself.

"G'day there. My name's Elizabeth." She was friendly looking and I welcomed the opportunity to speak English with someone new, other than Bill. It is funny how strange it feels when you no longer hear your native tongue being spoken on a daily basis. You begin to lose a part of your identity.

I smiled back and introduced myself. "Hi, I'm Kim, I am from Vancouver. How are you?"

"Pretty good thanks. But it's a bit muggy outside," she replied as she brushed her damp hair away from her face.

"Yeah, it takes a bit of getting used to, that's for sure. How do you like Japan?" I asked. I was always curious with regards to how other foreign women viewed their experience in this country.

"I love it. It's very beautiful. We have seen quite a few temples. But we are only travelling here for a couple of weeks and we are leaving very soon."

As we continued talking I learned that she was travelling throughout Asia with her husband. They had sold their home in Australia to finance their travel through Asia and North America. I explained that we had just arrived in Japan and we were looking to live and work in Japan teaching English but that we weren't sure where to find a job or where to live. Without hesitation she pulled out what looked like a passport from her waist pouch. I watched with curiosity as she held it out to me.

"We are leaving for the United States tomorrow. This is a rail pass for the Shinkansen, you know the bullet train that goes to Osaka? You can have this ticket if you like."

I was dumbstruck. I couldn't believe my luck or her kindness. It seemed like fate had provided us with yet another spontaneous opportunity and indeed this encounter would alter the course of our lives in Japan for better or worse. Here was, finally, a way out of Tokyo.

I thought quickly as to whether or not we had enough money to buy another ticket but I knew we didn't. "Wow, that is such a great opportunity, but I'm afraid we can't afford to buy a second ticket. We are down to our last few dollars........" I told her. I looked away in disappointment as I handed the ticket back to Elizabeth.

Without missing a beat, Elizabeth smiled reassuringly as she said, "No problem! I'll get my husband to give your boyfriend his pass and you can keep mine."

I looked at her with some skepticism but inside I was feeling like maybe our problems were solved. I looked at the ticket she had handed back to me and although there was a photo inside, there was just enough of a resemblance between Elizabeth and myself that it would probably go unnoticed. This ticket was worth the equivalent of US$250, which was a considerable sum for us. We said goodnight and I felt more relaxed than I had in several days. This beautiful gesture of goodwill from a complete stranger came as a wonderful surprise and I was beginning to learn that when you are alone in the world there will be times when you will need to rely on strangers for kindness and I vowed that whenever I had an opportunity to do the same I would. That young woman was an angel to me.

In the morning I met with Bill and told him about my talk with Elizabeth, expecting him to be excited at such a great opportunity. Instead he seemed concerned. How frustrating! I thought this was an opportunity we couldn't pass up and Bill was hesitating. It took me a whole day to finally convince him and time was running out because the tickets were going to expire in two more days and Elizabeth and her husband were leaving the next morning. In the end Bill wanted to explore a new city and agreed to the idea. We got the ticket from

Elizabeth's husband before they left and we were also soon on our way. We decided to leave behind the luggage that was still at Laura's and we would send for it later.

By that afternoon we had booked a time to travel on the Shinkansen. When we finally sat down in our seats I almost started crying from relief and excitement. It takes two and a half hours to get to Osaka on the Shinkansen and what amazed both of us was that the city sprawled the entire length of the island. Occasionally there were patches of green with only a few houses scattered around but mainly the buildings followed the train line all the way down to Osaka, with monstrous apartment buildings housed right beside rice fields.

~

Osaka City is located within Osaka Prefecture and is spread out over the Kansai Plain and runs north to south, with the ocean on the west and Kyoto towards the northeast. It is the second largest city on Honshu Island and in the early 90's was home to over 13 million people in an area half the size of the Lower Mainland of British Columbia in Canada. The main train that runs through the city is the Midosuji Subway. It starts in Senri-Chuo, the northernmost part of Osaka prefecture and runs through the downtown sector and finally ends in the south part of Osaka City. Although Osaka is a modern metropolis in its own right, it differs from Tokyo in size. Osaka is known for certain foods that originate in the region including *okonomiyaki,* which is a Japanese style pizza. There are many variations of this side dish, but a popular one is made of frying and pressing fried cabbage on a grill and then adding mayonnaise, bacon and squid for flavour. Though I could never stand the smell of this pizza it became one of Bill's favourite foods while in Japan. Other notable things about Osaka are its famous Osaka Aquarium, one of the largest in the world which houses a rare spotted porpoise whale. In the center of Osaka there is a famous castle affectionately known as *Osaka-jo.* It is a castle that was built originally in 1583 by Hideyoshi Toyotomi. The castle is famous for its historical background and its commanding view over the city. The castle was subsequently rebuilt several times after sustaining damage through fires and destruction resulting from damage during the Imperial Restoration. It suffered further damage from bombings over the city in World War II. Osaka is geographically linked with Kyoto, a city famous around the world for its preserved temples, untouched by the bombings of World War II. Kyoto is also famous for its geisha districts and even today, though there are far fewer practicing geisha, they can still be seen walking around in their gorgeous and expensive kimonos throughout areas of Kyoto. Perhaps one of my favourite things about Osaka were the trees which would bloom with white flowers, similar to a Canadian dogwood tree. The trees would produce an utterly gorgeous scent that smelled like fresh, ripe peaches, during the early part of fall. I fell in love with the distinct aroma as it encircled our neighbourhood but sadly I never learned the name of the tree. It would be here, in the city of Osaka, where we would make our home for the next two years.

After leaving the Shinkansen train we looked for the Midosuji subway which would take us to the northern part of the prefecture to Toyonaka City. There was a youth hostel in the municipality of *Ryokuchi-koen*, or 'green park', that we were going to stay at for a few nights. Dragging our luggage through the park we came upon the youth hostel, set on a small hill overlooking the vastness of the park. We found our way fairly easily and stopped in the park for a rest. The heat and humidity were incredible and we were becoming dehydrated after pulling our suitcases so far on foot. As we reached the top of the hill, the last wheel broke on our suitcases and we nearly collapsed from exhaustion.

We entered the hostel, sweaty and thirsty. I took in the cubicles against the far wall filled with slippers and thought how there was no way they would fit Bill's size 11 feet. At the desk, the young man could not find our names. We had called ahead of time to reserve beds but somehow we were not listed. Perhaps the look on my face changed his mind for as I was about to sit down and have a good cry out of sheer exhaustion, he suddenly found beds for us. Apparently, the youth hostel in Ryokuchi-koen is popular to many Japanese people and even schoolchildren and their teachers stay there during overnight excursions. After we were assigned our rooms we removed our shoes and found slippers to wear. This is perhaps one of the most well-known Japanese customs but it is very important and to wear your outside shoes indoors would be hugely discourteous and in some cases it would be grounds for being denied admittance into a building. We had too much luggage with us to fit into the small rooms so we had to leave our fan and a couple of suitcases in the hostel office. It was now getting dark and Bill and I decided to take a walk around the park.

The park was huge with a fish pond, rose garden, tennis courts, and bike paths winding in and out of the trees. We had a rare moment of quiet without hordes of people around us and we sat down on a bench, enjoying the rare moment of serenity.

"Are you happy that we came to Osaka?" Bill asked me. I sensed that he really wanted to know.

I smiled up at him as I answered, "Yes, I am. I'm really glad we came here. I like it so much better than Tokyo. Not to mention this park here, this whole area is really beautiful. Can you believe it?"

Bill just smiled and nodded. He saw what I was seeing. Here was a place that seemed an oasis in an otherwise unending concrete jungle. I think we both were feeling that this would be a good place to find a job and a place to live and then we would be set. Bill was concerned about finding work though. We had been in Japan for nearly 3 weeks and we had not received a suitable job offer.

Pensively, he looked out at the setting sun. "We better find jobs soon," he said quietly. His mood was serious and I knew as well what was at stake.

"Look Bill, we can look in tomorrow's paper. We'll find something, I mean we just got here."

As he held me on the bench, we heard soft voices murmuring behind us. I stiffened immediately, thinking that someone was spying on us. It turned out we were right. A group of young men were watching us through some bushes. Whatever their purpose, I was angry at not even being able to relax for one moment in this country! Privacy would become a memory.

23

As our moment of peace was shattered we decided to get up and retreat back to our rooms in the youth hostel. I hugged him good-bye in the lobby which was so hard to do and then he headed off to the men's section while I went in the other direction towards the women's section.

The next morning we were up early and Bill and I met in the lounge area which consisted of two vinyl couches styled from the 1960's and a stack of newspapers. Within a couple of minutes I spotted an ad that looked perfect for the two of us. A company in downtown Osaka was looking for two ESL instructors. I made the call and had an interview lined up for the next day. The timing was serendipitous as our Shinkansen tickets were going to expire within a couple of days and if we did not find jobs in that time we knew we would have to head back to Tokyo to retrieve our luggage and try our luck up there once again. The evening passed agonizingly slow but early the next morning we were up and out, heading back to the Midosuji subway. What a relief it was to take the train without being burdened with heavy luggage! We boarded the train at Ryokuchi-koen station and got off at Shinsaibashi station. From there it was chaos as we tried to follow directions, anxiously looking for a brown-bricked building on the corner of a street. The signs were in kanji so we could not read them and we had to rely on visual descriptions of landmarks in order to find our way. It seemed like we had been walking for hours and the morning wore on as the sun came up and we began sweating. Finally, we found the building but we were so early, despite getting lost, that the office wasn't open yet.

Now that we knew where the company was we decided to take a walk and explore the area. It was a commercial section with office buildings as far as you could see. We continued walking and came upon what is known as Den-Den town. It is a cornucopia of shops selling electronics sold at bargain prices. It's like a massive flea market with independent retailers competing for business.

As the time neared for our interview, we headed back to the building and walked up to the office of the Interac Language Institute. We were met by a charming young Japanese woman named Yuka who was very sweet and polite to us as she efficiently guided us in, offered us seats and handed us our application forms. Within half an hour we were hired for the job of teaching conversational English to Japanese businessmen. There was little to do beyond prove our natural ability to speak the English language and show that we were professionally presentable with some teaching background. Bill had taught drafting classes at the Professional Vocational Institute in B.C. back in the early 80's. My teaching background consisted of teaching soccer games and hosting birthday parties for children at my local recreation center. The salary range depended on your education and teaching background and Bill and I were both given a starting salary of ¥250,000.00 each per month, equivalent to about CDN$2200.00. We signed a one year contract and the company would act as our sponsors while we were living in Japan. We were to start the following week but because I had experience in office work I was asked to come in for a couple of days that week to help do some office work. We were so relieved! We were now legally able to stay and work in Japan for a whole year!

CHAPTER 2

Surviving Illness and Finding a Home

People were everywhere in the youth hostel, old and young alike. We approached the desk hoping to secure a few more nights until we could find a place to live. The supervisor explained to us that the hostel was booked full and that we would have to find somewhere else to stay for four nights. We contacted another hostel in south Osaka and reserved beds. Because we had a long trip ahead of us on the subway to the other hostel we arranged to leave much of our luggage in the Ryokuchi-koen youth hostel and head for our new temporary 'home' in Nagai.

The youth hostel in Nagai was very different from Ryokuchi-koen. It was much bigger and the surrounding area was flat with few trees. It seemed less hospitable and when Bill and I arrived it was a long while before we were able to register. The rooms were crowded, with people hanging clothing and towels out the windows making it look and feel like a refugee camp. In the cafeteria I spotted a woman coming up and carrying on in an exasperated tone as she watched us eat our rice. Suddenly the room became quiet and I sensed something unpleasant was about to occur. The woman grabbed our bowls away from us, replaced them again and gestured abruptly that we were to eat the rice without the soya sauce. Apparently it was not a good idea to empty half a bottle of soy sauce into your rice bowl! We had committed our first social *faux pas*, the first of many. I was feeling anxious to get away from the austerity and monotony of the youth hostel and I looked forward to working the next day.

I made it on my own to the school, separated for the first time from Bill. The office was busy with teachers, salesmen and administrative staff bustling about. I was introduced to many people and then assigned to taping narratives for English lessons. The first foreigner that I met that day was a young man named Peter, a balding, thin man with the look of an intellectual. He was a fellow Canadian who had been in Japan for nearly five years. He was now the supervisor for all instructors and he did his best to explain some of the workings of the company. The day went by quickly and I was excited about my new job.

The next few days flew quickly by and Bill and I returned to Ryokuchi-koen each evening with happiness. On the morning of our first official day of working as teachers, we went together to the office for an orientation with other teachers who had just arrived in Japan. We were informed by the branch manager, Masa, that we were all being sent to Tokyo the following week for teacher training at the head office of Interac. At the meeting, we also learned that we were going to have our travel visas processed by the national immigration department while we were there. We were then given a full tour of the Osaka office facilities and we had some time to speak with each other and find out where everyone was from. Together with Bill and I, there were a young couple from California who would be going to Tokyo to teach permanently and there were several more people already in Tokyo who would be coming to the Osaka branch to work.

The day had been long and later that night we looked forward to a good night's sleep. I was sharing my hostel room with two girls from Tokyo who were visiting and sightseeing in Osaka and Kyoto. They gave me a small souvenir from Osaka-jo, and as I looked at the little ceramic castle in my hand I felt touched by their generosity. I said goodnight to them but I felt guilty that I had nothing to give them in return. I had brought some Canadian coins with me but they were with all of our Canadian souvenirs still in our luggage in Tokyo.

I had fallen into a deep sleep when suddenly I was jolted awake by a throbbing pain in my lower back. At first I thought the bed was too hard as it was really only a wooden plank with a thin army style pad on top and so I figured I must have been sleeping in an uncomfortable position. I tried to sleep again but the pain came back stronger. After a couple of minutes the pain increased even more and I knew then that something was wrong. I was on the top bunk and I struggled to sit up. Sitting upright only exacerbated my pain but I knew I needed to get medical attention as soon as I could so I struggled to climb down the bunk ladder. As my back seized up in pain I momentarily let go of the ladder and fell to the floor waking the two girls sleeping near me. The girls were now wide awake, sitting on the edge of their bunks and staring at me. I looked helplessly into their faces, unable to communicate to them what was happening or to ask them to get help. They were visibly upset but made no move to get help. Finally, with the pain in my back becoming unbearable, I realized I had to get to Bill on my own but when I attempted to stand I collapsed from the pain which seemed to be worsening. Sobbing, I then began to crawl down the hallway toward the lobby. I tried in vain to get on my feet once more but the pain prevented me from doing this. When I reached the lobby I began calling out Bill's name in desperation. I kept calling and calling but no one came. I slid along the wooden floor on my hands and knees and collapsed halfway down the hall in a flood of tears. I lay there for a minute or two when finally the supervisor came running towards me. Seeing that I was ill he carried me to the couch and then he went running to get Bill. Bill came stumbling out of his room in a panic.

"What's wrong?" he called out.

"Bill, ...help me," I whispered. "Something's wrong, my back hurts bad and I can't stand up."

Bill knelt down beside me and tried to calm me down. The supervisor understood a little English and offered to call an ambulance. Terrified of any unknown horrors that a Japanese hospital might hold I shook my head. I lay there for perhaps an hour as the pain gradually subsided. It wasn't gone altogether, but it was less severe and I felt I could manage until the morning when we could contact the company we worked for and get their help. Bill and I spent the rest of the night together, my head in his lap, with the supervisor worriedly resting nearby. I was grateful for the man's compassion in allowing us to stay together. In the morning I felt well enough to get dressed and walk around on my feet. Leaving for the office, I felt the pain recurring and although I had briefly thought that it might go away I realized that I needed medical attention.

At the office I spoke to the administrator, Taeko, a very warm and friendly woman. She contacted a local doctor who was used to treating foreigners and she put Bill and I into a taxi. Along the way I squeezed Bill's hand nervously, anxious about what might be physically wrong with me, yet I was relieved that I would be getting help at last.

The doctor was located in a small building squeezed in between many other buildings on a very narrow back street. As soon as we approached the reception counter we were escorted into the doctor's office/examination room, past the other patients waiting in the hallway. It appeared that because we were foreigners, we were to be treated differently, which might explain the immediate treatment. I felt a sense of guilt for the patients who were ahead of me but I also realized that they just might want to get me in and out of here as fast as possible because I was a gaijin. The doctor was an older man with heavily wrinkled eyes that sparkled when he spoke. His English was broken and mispronounced but he was easily understood.

"Hello, hello. Please sit. My name Dr. Ito. You feel pain?" He gestured at my body.

I explained where I had felt the pain and that I thought it might be a kidney infection. He sent me away with the nurse who gave me a small container and she asked me to go into the washroom and ..." put urine into cup, please put in cup."

Afterwards, the doctor was sitting and examining my urine under a microscope while Bill and I waited opposite him. He then produced a bag of pills and confirmed that I had, indeed, a kidney infection. The pills were antibiotics and I was told that I should take them with juice or water and soon the pain would be gone. How relieved I was that I did not have to undergo major tests and that with the magic of pills I would be healthy again! The doctor looked at me and smiled, his eyes twinkled when he said to me "This man love you very much. He very worried for you."

I looked up at Bill, who had his arm around me, and I replied "I know."

Thanking the doctor and his nurse, we left the clinic and headed back to the office for more orientation meetings. I hugged Bill out of relief, out of love, and to reassure him that I was okay.

~

We were to leave for Tokyo in the afternoon. It had been a few days since my visit with Dr. Ito, whom I considered to be the second angel I had encountered in this country. I was feeling completely well again. We were waiting for the next Shinkansen train to Tokyo, fully paid for by the company. We never would have imagined that we would be taking the famous 'bullet' train twice in our first month in Japan. Our financial situation was so bad that we had been given money up front by the school for living expenses. Bill and I had been eating mainly pop, rice and raw vegetables, with the occasional meal at a restaurant. Although I had not yet acquired a taste for sushi I would have given anything to go into a nice restaurant and order a steak and salad. Those days were yet to come but for now we were living hand to mouth on borrowed money.

The train ride passed by uneventfully and once back in Tokyo we were assaulted with the sheer expanse of the city once again. The head office of Interac Language School was located in the center of Tokyo and we were by now becoming very adept at finding our way around the cities of Japan by train. With a little luck, a lot of determination and train maps, we were able to guide ourselves without the benefit of any signs in English. The Tokyo office was large and very austere when compared with the Osaka office. We were directed into a room where there were other foreign teachers bound for Osaka. We glanced around the room and saw two young women, a young couple and a middle-aged woman. We seated ourselves and waited to see what would happen next. Before we had a chance to talk to anyone, we were again led into a room, this time an enormous, banquet style room filled with more foreigners than we had seen since leaving Canada. The purpose of this 'mass meeting' was to acquaint ourselves with other English teachers, some of whom were experienced in the field and others, like Bill and I, who were new to the job. After spending about an hour talking to various people, the large group was divided into sub-groups, based upon the branches that people would be teaching at. Bill and I met up again with the young women and the couple and their friend. We learned that the young women were from New York and Washington D.C. and their names were Barbara and Lisa. The couple were from Boston and the other woman was from New Jersey.

We spent the afternoon discussing teaching techniques, the kind of people we would be teaching (mostly businessmen) and learning about materials we could use for our teaching. It was our first exposure to the world of ESL teaching. The school had paid for lodging for all teachers and Bill and I were to spend the next two nights at a *ryokan* in Tokyo. Ryokans are traditional bed and breakfast accommodations in Japan which offer rooms to stay in that are in Japanese homes. You can expect to sleep in a tatami room and you are provided with simple meals and beverages served at set times. Our ryokan was dark and narrow with intertwining hallways that wound in a maze-like manner heading to separate rooms. Our room consisted of a tiny area covered in tatami mats and furnished with a low table, cushions and a fan. There were lemon biscuits and tea laid out for our arrival. In the one adjoining room there were two futons for sleeping. There were no windows and it was like being in a bamboo prison. We spent very little time there except to bathe and sleep.

In the morning we were off to the Tokyo Immigration Department to get our work visas. The building was very contemporary and we found the immigration department on the 3rd floor. Inside there were many people lined up waiting for the office to open. There were a handful of Caucasians but mostly there were people from southern Asian countries. We waited, and as more people strolled in, the clerks behind the counter scurried about, shuffling papers and stamping documents. The whole process involved having our papers inspected and stamped and following approval, we were issued our Alien Registration cards which we were told to carry with us at all times. If we became involved in a conflict of any kind and the police discovered us without our Alien Registration card, then technically we could be hauled off to jail until our embassy located the proper papers. We didn't anticipate that we would have any conflicts but, nonetheless, I felt uneasy as I walked out of the building with Bill. Looking down at my Alien Registration card I snickered "Hey, I am now *officially* an alien!"

Bill glanced over at me. "That also means we don't have the rights here that we did at home," he informed me.

I pondered Bill's words but after shoving the card in my wallet my mind was already looking forward to working and getting ahead in Japan.

Our stay in Tokyo was short and busy but we managed to get enough free time from our schedule to travel to Yamato to visit with Laura and pick up our remaining luggage. Laura was busy teaching and we were only able to briefly catch up with each other on the events of the past few weeks. We arranged for our luggage to be shipped to Osaka and before long we were on our way back ourselves.

We had accomplished a great deal in the past three weeks but still we needed a place to live. Before I could really focus on working I needed the stability and comfort of my own place. Foreigners who are hired outside of Japan usually have their living arrangements made for them prior to their arrival in Japan. For us, the work had to be done ourselves. Aware of our language barrier, and the social custom of doing business in Japan with personal acquaintances only, I did expect apartment hunting to be challenging. It turned out to be an absolute nightmare.

First of all, you need a substantial damage deposit known as 'key' money in Japan. The amount is not standardized and each land-lord can charge what he or she wants and the money is not always returned. Bill and I were essentially broke and could not feasibly put up any key money. Our company, Interac, offered to loan us the money which would then be deducted from our monthly cheques. Once that was solved, we then set out to find a real estate agent. We already knew we wanted to live in Ryokuchi-koen because of its natural beauty. Also, it was only 40 minutes away by train from the school.

One afternoon we wandered into a real estate office off the street and were met with shocked stares and excited giggling from the receptionists.

"Ah! Gaijin!" the women squealed at us. They appeared to be very uncomfortable and not quite sure what to do with us. Although I was beginning to become accustomed to hearing this label it always felt disparaging and it didn't exactly make me feel accepted in this society. We stood for several minutes in the doorway of the office until finally one of the women had the presence of mind to gesture for us to sit down. Two glasses of iced tea were placed in front of us while the employees scurried about conferring with one another. They were obviously perplexed at having to deal with two gaijin who wandered in off the street.

Several moments later a young woman sat down in front of us and handed us a pad of paper. There being essentially no verbal communication possible, we resorted to drawing pictures of what we wanted. I drew a picture of a Japanese toilet and put a big "X" through it and then I drew a picture of a western toilet and circled it while nodding my head. The woman and her male colleague glanced down at the paper and seemed to understand. I then wrote '2 DK' on the paper, referring to two tatami rooms with a kitchen and dining area. I next wrote ¥60,000 - ¥80,000 as the amount that we were willing to pay for monthly rent. I also gave them the phone number of our office, realizing that we were going to need an interpreter.

I paused and took a sip of my tea while glancing over at Bill. Bill refused to drink his beverage even though it was very hot outside. The tea was not North American style iced tea but rather a bitter tea kept chilled and very popular in Japan during the summer months.

"Do you think they understand what we want?" I asked Bill.

"Hopefully, but probably not. We need to get them to talk to Taeko or Masa, there's gonna be paper work involved, it's not as simple as you think," he replied.

There then followed a discussion in Japanese and then the woman politely gestured for us to leave. We got up and left. I felt triumphant, thinking that I had accomplished the impossible.

It was a few days before we discovered that the people in the real estate office were willing to take us to look at apartments. Excited, we met the woman at the office we had gone to a few days earlier. She drove us around the city pointing out a couple of buildings. One was so run down on the outside that we indicated by a shake of our heads that we were unwilling to take a look inside. Another building seemed acceptable on the outside, but once inside, we noticed the linoleum was peeling up from the floor and there were cracks in the walls. I began to get very upset, thinking that because we were gaijin we were only being shown rundown apartments. It was an unsuccessful afternoon. Days later, the director of the school where we worked called to say that they had a nice apartment for us to look at in Ryokuchi-koen. Accompanying the woman from the real estate office once more, we drove a short distance from Ryokuchi-koen station along the highway beside a river and then we drove over a small bridge into a quiet little neighbourhood.

I looked up at a very modern looking but narrow three story concrete apartment building. Entering the apartment, it appeared new and clean, with nice bright windows and hardwood floors. The best part was that there was a western style bathroom, albeit the bathtub would be better suited for a toddler-sized adult. The colour scheme throughout was beige and white offset by the rich color of the wood floor in the kitchen. The other two rooms were covered with tatami mats and separated from the kitchen by heavy wood sliding doors. As I gazed around I knew I liked it but I had concerns. First of all, it was very small. There were no appliances, light fixtures or window coverings, never mind heating or air-conditioning. These necessities would be our responsibility. There was a sliding glass door that led to a small balcony outside. Stepping outside I could see apartment buildings to my left, a playground directly below and an elementary school across the street to my right. The apartment was shaped like a square box and it was an end unit. Directly below was a convenience store. In total, the apartment was about 400 square feet. Bill and I looked silently at each other.

"Bill, we have been looking at apartments for days. This is perfect. I don't want to look at anything else. This is it!" I suddenly felt my adrenaline going, I was excited. I carried on as though it was already ours, going from room to room in my excitement.

In the meantime we continued to stay at the youth hostel in Ryokuchi-koen, familiarizing ourselves with the area and what it had to offer. We knew it was an upper class neighbourhood judging by the lush, well-kept landscaping and the expensive Rolls-Royces parked outside the buildings. The area, we learned, was extremely popular among the urban professionals for its beauty and access to recreation. What we didn't know at the time, however, was that it was close to an area populated by the local bosozoku and yakuza gangs.

It was a crushing blow to learn a couple of days later that the owner of the building refused to accept foreign tenants. I was truly shocked and I despaired over the futility of our situation of living in a foreign land as a visible minority. It was a demeaning and frustrating experi-ence in prejudice that I had only heard or read about happening to other people. We had professional jobs, we were hard-working, hon-est people, yet the simple fact that we were immigrants labelled us and instantly created a barrier. We complained bitterly to the direc-tor of our school, not comprehending the unfairness of the situation. Since the school was acting as our sponsor while we were in the country, we hoped that they would help us. Despite our situation, and unknown to us, there were discussions going on between the landlord and our company director. Eventually, a deal was worked out, and the following day the director called and asked us to meet him at the apartment. Upon arriving at the apartment, we learned that we had been accepted.

We were to pay ¥800,000.00 in key money, the equivalent of US$6,000.00 It seemed like an enormous amount to pay and we asked if they would accept ¥400,000.00 on the condition that we would receive nothing back upon termination of the tenancy. The owner agreed and on September 4, 1989 we moved into our little apartment in Ryokuchi-koen, surrounded by a park, a river and an elementary school.

CHAPTER 3

Learning to Teach

With my illness and apartment hunting now out of the way, we settled into a new schedule of teaching. Bill and I were scheduled to teach our first classes at the same company, Aoki Kintetsu, a major construction firm with a contract to build the new International Osaka Airport. It was six stops away on the Midosuji subway followed by a twenty minute walk to the company's building. I was assigned the lower level class and Bill had the advanced students. My class was comprised of six company men and one secretary. The older men seemed to be not too interested in being in English language classes and they were unfocused on the lessons. They peppered me with personal questions, such as my age or what my breast size was. The only way I could deal with that was to either ignore the questions or fire it right back in a gender related way. At the age of twenty-two, I considered myself to be the ultimate professional and had not yet learned how to relax and go with the moment. This only caused more tension and I would struggle to keep control of the class and keep the students motivated to learn. The commitment level of the students was weak at best and I could only shake my head when some students walked in half an hour late for a one hour class. The way I looked at it, I also had to get up early to be there for 7:30 a.m. so why couldn't they? It would be a short while later that I would learn about the 'work' after work, where men would often be encouraged to join their co-workers and sometimes their supervisors for many hours of drinking. After learning this, I became more sympathetic to the late arrivals to my class. There was an aspect to this subculture though that I found very disturbing - on many occasions as Bill and I would be sleeping, we would be awoken in the middle of the night by the awful sound of men vomiting on their way home from their drinking. In the mornings, it was not unusual to find what many Japanese refer to as 'sidewalk pizza' splattered here and there.

Gradually, other classes were assigned to us and soon our early mornings and evenings were completely booked. Classes were generally taught during these hours to accommodate the business people who were our students. Some companies we taught at provided us with students that were genuinely interested and hard working. Other companies were merely subjecting their employees to an hour or so of torture. We found that the employees who had a choice to join in on the classes were more consistent with their attendance and they were the ones who learned the most. Those students who were ordered to attend merely sat vacantly, watching the minutes pass by. Most classes were taught using our school's official English textbook. Although the grammar and vocabulary lessons were laid out in simple terms, the context was uninteresting. I began to search out and design my own material, becoming very creative at lesson planning.

There seemed to be no standardized methods of teaching. I knew of some teachers who were merely handing out crosswords (of their own admission) and accompanying their students to bars. While I envied the idea of freedom and the spontaneous fun this way of teaching entailed, I preferred to earnestly teach by thinking lessons through beforehand with a set goal in mind for each class. I came to believe that relying only on general conversation could become a struggle and a bore after awhile and that a concrete lesson plan was needed. So it was that initially I spent much of my free time at the school, planning and preparing lessons and filling in attendance sheets. It also provided me with the opportunity to meet and talk with other teachers.

There was an eclectic assortment of foreigners working for our company. There were several people from Canada and the U.S. as well as Britain, Australia and even India. It was during one such afternoon as I sat planning a lesson when two young guys sauntered over to the table.

"Hello. You a kiwi girl?" the blonde one asked me. Before I had a chance to react, the brunette responded "Nah, she's a Canuck that one. Her mate is here with her somewhere."

"Well, you're both right, I guess. I am Canadian, and I'm here with my fiancé. His name is Bill. Mine is Kim. Where are you two from? Let me guess...Australia, right?" I waited for their reaction.

"Well, now *that's* a good guess. Nice to meet you. My name's Andy and this is my brother B.J.," said the blonde one as he pointed to his brother. They both sat down on either side of me and they pulled out their partially filled in attendance sheets.

"How long have you guys been here?" I asked.

Andy dabbed his stamp in the ink blotter. "Oh, about 3 months I would say. We'll stay about a year, then head back," he answered. I watched as he busily kept stamping, not looking up.

I looked over at Andy's dark haired brother. "B.J., right? So, what do you think of living here?" I asked.

"It's alright. Lots of good clubs, the money is not too bad. Just don't like the commuting," he said. I studied both men and they seemed to be genuinely friendly, very laid back with a sharp sense of humour.

"Where are you guys living at?" I was curious to find out as there seemed to be no foreigners in our area.

"We live at the southeast end, near Namba," Andy informed me. He finished stamping and looked over at me.

"How about you and...Bill, right? Whereabouts do you guys live?" he asked.

"Well, after we stayed at the youth hostel in Ryokuchi-koen, we fell in love with the area and so we found a small place nearby. It's nice and new but it's *really* small."

As we continued talking, the two young girls , Barbara and Lisa, whom we had first met in Tokyo, walked in and we all began talking about everything from good restaurants to how long we were staying. It felt so good to be speaking English again in a group! We made plans to get together socially. There was a shrine festival coming up in the southern city of Kishiwada in Fukuyama prefecture, south of Osaka, that a few of us decided to attend. Our little group of teachers would become a great support network during our stay in Japan. With about ten of us going, we had plans to meet up with everyone at the Namba train station.

On the day of the festival, it was very hot and muggy as I scurried around the apartment trying to find something to wear. I ended up choosing a pale blue cotton sundress that would be light and airy in the oppressive heat. Outside, we had a twenty minute walk to the train station and every step I took resulted in large beads of sweat dripping down the entire front of my body. I wished so badly for a bike or a scooter at that point. Most of the teachers we worked with lived either in south Osaka or further out near Kyoto. We had to travel about an hour before we would meet up with them. We were the first to arrive at Namba station in Osaka City and we waited for the others to join us. A short while later the two girls from the States arrived with the brothers from Australia. We waited together for the others and eventually they arrived and we headed down to Kishiwada, a two hour train ride away.

The festival involved wooden shrines being pulled along the streets by young men. Each shrine represented a separate district and the participants wore brightly coloured clothing carrying swords in their waists. I watched in fascination with the others as the men danced on top of the narrow shrines. The men were required to race each other several times a day for three days with only brief resting periods. Every year, we were told, there were men killed, trampled under the weight of a shrine as it toppled over. The workmanship on the shrines was incredible with intricate carvings that dated back in some cases hundreds of years. We stood on the edge of the street after being warned that spectators were also sometimes injured during the festival. The air was thick with humidity and we stood squeezed up within the mass of people waiting for the parade of shrines. We eagerly anticipated the crashing sound of wood splintering and the cries of the men. Instead we saw trained performers sitting astride the shrines waving and dancing in a rhythmic, warrior-like manner.

The afternoon wore on and we were becoming hungry and tired. One of the salesmen from our company invited us to his parent's home for lunch. Moto led us down a few side streets and then into a typical apartment building. Their apartment was halfway up but the greatest joy was that it was air-conditioned! Moto served us drinks and sandwiches and he was very polite and friendly. We gratefully relaxed in the apartment, flaking out on the couches and talking about the events of the day.

"Those shrines were beautiful, so old," Lisa said.

"The men were so muscular but good dancers too," I added.

Moto leaned over to take a sip of his tea. "This festival is very famous here in Japan. This year, very lucky, no one killed," he stated.

We continued on gabbing about our impressions of the festival when I began to tire and so Bill and I thanked Moto for his warm hospitality and we left. I was totally worn out from the heat. We caught the train back home and collapsed several hours later in exhaustion in our little apartment without air-conditioning. The whir of the fan lulled us into a deep sleep.

The weather had finally begun to cool by the end of September and it was nice to be able to walk outside without becoming drenched in sweat. Another weekend had arrived and we had some free time so we decided to check out a restaurant that Andy and B.J. had recommended. The restaurant was located under the Osaka Hilton Hotel at Umeda station. We now had our own bank accounts and strangely, in an economically powerful country such as Japan, you could only access banking machines during business hours. It was pointless to try to withdraw money later in the day. We needed money for our dinner, so Bill offered to go to the bank and come home before we left. I kept telling him to get going because the banks closed at 2:00 p.m. but he insisted they were open until 3:00 p.m. Finally he left while I did our laundry in the bathtub. We did not have any furniture or modern appliances so daily living tasks were tedious. I waited for him to come back and wondered what was taking him so long. I was outside hanging the clothes on a piece of twine strung from one end of the balcony to the other, when I heard the front door slam shut. I turned to go in and I saw Bill sitting on the floor looking anywhere but at me.

"The bank was closed," he mumbled quietly.

I could feel my pulse quicken and I silently wondered how we could survive for two days without money or food.

"See, I told you they closed at 2:00 p.m.! Now what are we going to do for money?" I yelled. I couldn't believe this was happening.

My disbelief and shock overwhelmed me. "Bill, we don't have any food in the fridge, the school is closed for the weekend...I just can't believe this is happening! Just what are we supposed to do?"

I walked back and forth becoming more scared than angry. Bill sat silently, waiting for me to calm down, obviously just as worried as I was.

"What about your Visa?" he finally asked.

"Look, you know it expired a month ago!" I shouted at him.

"Well, maybe we can try to use it anyway," he suggested.

"Yeah, well listen here Clyde, Bonnie here doesn't want to go to jail!" I flipped back.

Without any other choice presenting itself before us, I knew we had to try to use my expired Visa because we had to eat. I got myself ready and we left.

The restaurant was done up inside an actual caboose which had been imported from San Francisco. It was designed in an old western style and the employees spoke perfect English. We were seated in a private booth and we poured over the menu, our appetites huge for familiar food. We each ordered the prime rib steak and salad bar, feeling like convicts who were about to eat their last meal. The food was delicious with a huge variety of fresh fruits and vegetables in the salad bar. Thinking that we needed to fill ourselves up as much as possible, we both ordered cheesecake for dessert. At the end of the meal we lingered over coffee, nervous about paying. Finally, I placed my expired Visa card on the table and waited for the waiter to take it away. We waited quietly, expecting him to return and demand another form of payment. But the waiter came back and handed me the slip to sign. I signed it and we left the restaurant with a huge sense of relief. About a month later I received my Visa statement in the mail from my bank in Canada and eventually I was able to pay it off completely. Because the school paid for our transportation, we had train passes and didn't have to worry about getting around for the rest of the weekend. We had just enough money to buy some pop and chips for food for the next day. After this experience, Bill never forgot what time the banks closed each day!

The week before we had discovered a modern department store called Tokyu Hands near our apartment. A lot of the items were hand-made and you could buy craft supplies and other different items. We ended up buying a couple of puzzles for entertainment on quiet days and so one Sunday we spent part of the day doing the puzzles and spent the later part of the afternoon walking through the park. As we walked through the garden area we spotted the tennis courts that we had first seen when we had stayed at the nearby youth hostel and we decided we would buy some rackets and balls and start playing. Soon after, we began heading over to the courts to play a game or two. It wasn't long before we started to draw a crowd of curious onlookers, studying our moves and game strategies.

I couldn't help laughing. "I sure hope they don't think we're Chris Evert or Andre Agassiz!" I said.

Each time we showed up to play a game of tennis, we would inevitably look up to find a sea of faces peeking at us through the bushes. At first I tried to find the humour in our situation.

"We should actually put out some signs and start charging people to watch, don't you think?" I asked Bill. He would grin at the hilarity of our newfound celebrity status. But there came a day when I could no longer relax and concentrate on the game so our new pastime soon went by the wayside.

The remainder of September passed quickly by and the fall season was upon us. I became very self-conscious about my appearance as the weeks wore on as I felt my clothes and overall look were too obvious a representation of my lack of spending money. The Japanese women were impeccably dressed and beautiful to look at, with their tiny slim figures and long black hair. Their make-up was flawless and they were so perfectly dressed that they resembled mannequins. I felt insignificant with my cheaply made Canadian clothes. I had only brought a handful of professional outfits and most were made of thin material suitable for warmer months. Clothing in Japan seemed incredibly expensive yet I hungered to go shopping.

One particular day when Bill and I were exploring a commercial area of Osaka City, I wandered into a shoe store in one of the underground malls. I saw a pair of brown suede low-heeled shoes for about ¥2,900 or CDN$25.00. Bill was adamantly opposed to spending any money unnecessarily given our financial circumstances. My viewpoint was that I was young and working like crazy so why couldn't I buy a pair of shoes? I was annoyed and decided to buy them anyway. The store clerk found my size which turned out to be the largest size they had. I looked closely at the numbers on the bottom of the shoe and noted that I was a size 25.5, equivalent to an eight and a half. I left the store triumphantly, my new shoes in hand, and walked past Bill who was still angry with me. It was to become a source of conflict between the two of us even though I was earning my own money. Bill wanted to work and save while I wanted to work and spend, caught up in the pressure of needing to feel pretty and feminine in a country full of beautiful women. Many of these women seemed to be very interested in Bill and it was hard for me to witness them shamelessly flirt with him even in my presence. For some reason, we had noticed that many Japanese women were attracted to western men and the western men were equally fawning over the Japanese women. Historically in Japan, like elsewhere, young people generally married for economic and social purposes. Marriages were often arranged and some couples would, in time, come to love each other. This social ritual has also occurred in many other cultures throughout the world in the past, often out of necessity, for tribal survival. But times, we were told, were changing in Japan too, although at a slower pace than in Europe and North America. It appeared that Japanese women were seeking out western men in the belief that they would be less patriarchal and more chivalrous.

At the beginning of October, Bill and I were invited out for the evening by our students from Aoki Kintetsu, a large construction company. We were treated to a lavish dinner at a hotel in downtown Umeda, a shopping district of Osaka. The meal was delicious and we dined on seafood, meat, chicken, sushi, noodles and salads. The conversation was lively as we shared bottles of red wine, produced by the owner of the hotel.

Afterwards, my female student, Kazue, leaned over towards me. "Kim, would you like to go to drinking club after or go home?" she asked politely.

I looked at her quizzically for a moment. I wasn't sure. I hadn't expected to go out to a club later but the evening was unfolding nicely and we were having a good time. I looked over at Bill.

"It's your decision," I told him. At Bill's nod of the head I agreed. Turning back to Kazue I smiled and nodded. "Sure, sounds like a great idea!" I answered her.

I noticed a look of mild displeasure cross Kazue's face and I wondered if maybe she was tired and wanted to go home and that perhaps she was merely being polite by inviting us out.

"You know, Kazue, we don't have to go out. Or, if you would like to go home, please do. I don't want to impose on you. Whatever you decide is okay with us," I told her.

Kazue responded swiftly and reassured us that she would come with us and that she was fine. Still, an inner voice told me something else was going on here beneath the surface. For the moment I shrugged it off and we headed outside to a taxi where a group of us clambered in as the driver stood by with his white gloved hands. Once we were all in, the driver got behind the wheel, hit a switch and the doors automatically closed.

The club we were brought to was a privately owned hostess bar which businessmen frequent after work. It was very expensive and as a rule only certain employees can enjoy this privilege which is essentially company paid entertainment. We learned, as we descended the stairs into a comfy looking bar/lounge, that the cost to enter was about US$200.00 per person. I looked around and saw a small room with a white sectional sofa and some glass coffee tables. Opposite the sofa was a small bar lining the wall and it was clearly well stocked. There were bowls of popcorn and candy on the tables. Music was play-ing softly in the background and sexy, attractive young women began pouring drinks for the few men that were there. Then it donned on me why the cover charge was so steep. These women were not your average cocktail waitresses, rather they were employed strictly for the pleasure of the male patrons.

One of my other students, Kenichi, clearly in a pleasurable mood, motioned for me to sit beside Kazue, who looked absolutely miser-able. I sat beside her, now feeling uneasy and guilty for causing her to be here on this night and even though it was she who invited us I could see that she was merely the messenger in this situation. I was waiting for Bill to join us but he was led to another sofa and seated beside a hostess. I noticed the woman stand up and then promptly sit on Bill's lap. I sat there, completely stunned. This must be a joke I thought as I felt my heart race. Unfortunately, as I watched, it became clear that Kenichi was serious about Bill enjoying himself while I was expected to play the role of hapless victim. I had been having trouble with Kenichi in class. He was often rude and disruptive to the point that I had to ask him to leave the class one day. As I was now learn-ing, I had humiliated him and he was now enjoying humiliating me.

Kenichi tried to get my attention. "This bar is very expensive," he informed me proudly. He then sat down beside a hostess. "These girls are here for *my* pleasure. Do you believe me?" he asked with a smirk.

I chose not to respond, partly because I was in shock and partly because I didn't know if I could control what might come out of my mouth at that moment. I continued to sit in silence, my ears and cheeks burning red, unable to speak but feeling close to tears.

"Look over here," Kenichi commanded as he gestured at the girl sitting on his lap. "I can take off her blouse and touch her breast!" he smiled broadly. "Do you want me to show you?" He reached for her blouse and I spoke up quickly.

"No, that is not necessary," I said. I glanced over at Bill who was sitting, also smiling, as the hostess poured whisky into his glass and lit his cigarette. I nearly jumped out of my seat when I saw her putting popcorn into his mouth. She dropped a piece, which fell into her lap and I watched in shock as Bill leaned down and picked it up off her lap. She giggled and let her long hair fall over Bill's face. I was clearly in a bad situation and beginning to unravel. Had I been at home in Canada it would have been easy to call a cab and leave. Here, in a strange part of the city, a young woman alone at night and unable to speak a word of Japanese, I knew I could not just leave on my own. I looked over at Kazue who seemed unable to meet my gaze, as though she knew how this was going to play out. I glanced again at Bill, who was by now hopelessly drunk.

After perhaps an hour, maybe two, Kazue ventured that it might be a good time to leave. I was grateful for her initiative but wondered why it took her so long, seeing my discomfort. I was angry at myself as well, for having been so passive and unable to stop this behaviour. As we left and walked outside, the tears began streaming down my face. I strode ahead of the group, disgusted with how the evening had turned out. I was angry with Bill for participating so willingly and for Kenichi for being so cruel and vindictive. I walked faster to get away from the men and eventually Kazue caught up with me and assisted me in waving over a taxi, giving the driver my address.

"I am sorry Kim, for what happened tonight. Very sorry," she whispered. She looked so sad. She said good night and turned away.

I didn't respond. I was so numb with hurt and anger that I just sat frozen in my seat. How was I going to face these people again? How could I possibly speak to Kenichi again? It was all I could do to keep from slapping him earlier. It was only because we were in a foreign country and our behaviour was so important that I controlled myself. But it was a high price to pay for my pride and feelings. It took me a long time to forgive Bill and truly recover from that night. Needless to say, I spoke to the company manager soon after, and explained what had happened and that Kenichi was no longer welcome in my class and I never saw him again.

I did see Kazue again, however, and she had a chance to explain to me that Kenichi was a troubled man who flouted his cultural control over women, and that when I showed up on the scene, he found it intolerable that a women half his age would be in a position of authority over him and he was unable to accept it.

That whole event had been difficult, but again I eventually chalked it up to a life learning lesson and I realized that there are good and bad people everywhere and that bad people suffer their own problems too.

CHAPTER 4

Christmas Alone

By November of 1989 the weather was bitterly cold. We had only our ski jackets to wear and the apartment had no heat. Mornings were spent dashing from the warmth of our futon into a steaming hot shower and getting dressed as quickly as possible. It was a long walk from our apartment to the train station and while wearing heels and a ski jacket made me look ridiculous it also did not protect my legs from freezing. So one afternoon as Bill and I were walking in one of the underground malls, I spotted a store selling winter coats. I walked in, expecting only to browse for a minute, thinking the prices would be beyond my means when I came across a white cashmere full length coat. I was shocked to discover the price tag showing ¥5,000.00! For less than fifty dollars I would be able to look the part of a young professional teacher, but most importantly I would be warm. Walking out of the store, wearing my new coat, I felt like Cinderella. To be finally warm was a remarkable gift. That coat was one of the most important and memorable purchases I ever made in Japan.

Although I was now warm and cozy with my new winter coat, living in the apartment without central heat was becoming a real problem. It was very cold and we bundled up in sweaters and extra pairs of socks trying to keep warm. As winter approached, and the air became bitingly cold, we struggled to stay comfortable. One evening, on his way home from teaching, Bill spotted a gomi heater on the sidewalk. Wasting no time, he carried it into the apartment to share his newfound treasure with me. I gazed skeptically at the rusty old heater, wondering if it would be safe to use and that there was most likely a reason why it was sitting in the garbage pile on the street. Bill assured me that it would work fine and I knew that we couldn't really afford to go out and buy a new one. Because it was a kerosene heater, it would be very effective in keeping our little place warm throughout the winter. That very night, Bill got the heater working, and despite the fact that it gave off a bit of a smell, within minutes the rooms were warmed up and the air temperature rose sharply. It felt so good to be warm again! We removed our sweaters and lounged on our futons, completely relaxed. Just before we went to sleep, Bill opened the bedroom window a crack so that some of the smell could blow outside and fresh air could get in. At some point in the middle of the night, Bill woke up because he heard me coughing. Instantly, he slid open the window all the way, letting in fresh air. Trying to shake me awake, he kept calling my name , over and over.

"Kim! Kim! Wake up......open your eyes!" he was yelling as loud as he could.

Still getting no reaction, he kept yelling my name. I remember suddenly opening my eyes, coughing uncontrollably, to see him hovering over me. I was groggy and confused, trying to wake up and unable to stop coughing. Bill carried me over to the balcony and kept me sitting upright, letting the outside air fill my lungs. Once he was sure that I was fully awake, he told me to stay sitting by the balcony and not to go back to sleep. He turned off the heater, and took it outside, carrying it back down the steps and putting it right back on the sidewalk where he found it.

It was a scary incident, and I was thankful that Bill had the foresight to keep that window open a crack, enabling at least some fresh air to get inside. Bill always said that it was my coughing that had caused him to wake up. We were incredibly lucky that we didn't succumb to carbon monoxide poisoning.

Although I was relieved to be rid of that belching, smoking death trap, we were now back to having a freezing apartment. Heaters were expensive and any spare money, of which there was little, was being squirreled away for bikes. There was just no extra money for a heater. Deciding that it was a necessity we couldn't survive without, we dipped into our next paycheque, and then spent a free day heading to Den-Den town to buy a new heater. We were beyond excited at the thought of having heat, but it would mean that we would need to cut down on meals for a few weeks and eat as cheaply as we could. Rice and noodles became our staple diet for quite awhile.

Bill's parents were coming to Japan to visit us after a trip to Hong Kong. They were going to visit Laura in Tokyo first and then head down to see us in Osaka. They were to stay with us for four days. When the day of their arrival came, Bill met them after one of his classes at a Shinkansen platform near Kyoto. The feeling of seeing familiar faces after so many months of isolation was overwhelming. Bob and Donna were eager to see some of the sights in Kyoto so we booked a few days off and headed to the ancient city to view some of the temples.

Bill, his parents and I, visiting the Osaka Castle

Among the most beautiful of the temples is Kiyomizu-dera, which sits high on a hilltop overlooking the city. Built in 1633, the main part of the temple is entirely structured out of wood without a single nail. I found this feat of architecture and construction quite amazing. When you compare the importance of construction from the older periods to modern times it is interesting how attitudes have changed. For young Japanese people today, construction work is seen as dirty and is very unpopular. At the temple there is a path marked with a large boulder at one end. It is known as the fertility walk. Along with some Japanese schoolgirls, I closed my eyes and attempted to walk in a straight line towards the stone. Much to my embarrassment and shock I walked right off the path and into a wall! Opening my eyes, I stepped back onto the path and continued walking toward the stone. I wasn't going to let a little detour prevent me from reaching my goal.

We finished viewing the temple and then we walked down the hill lined with little tourist shops that sold everything from deep fried maple leaves to pottery. It was a serene setting and we relaxed despite the chill in the air as we ate rice burgers and beer.

Kyoto is a very pretty city, surrounded by mountains and full of historic neighbourhoods lining the many estuaries running throughout the city. The atmosphere had a quiet stillness with a stunning backdrop of hillsides dotted with temples. There were also many ryokans and teahouses scattered throughout the city. We would come back many times to visit Kyoto on weekends and it always held the same appeal as if seeing it for the first time all over again.

With Bill's parents needing to be kept busy seeing the sights, we decided to take them on a tour of Osaka Castle. In the courtyard there was an older man with a bicycle full of trinkets and letters that had been sent to him from tourists he had spoken with throughout the years. He called himself the 'Ambassador of the World' and he spent much of his time meeting with foreigners and talking about Japan. He was very interesting and friendly and we ended up having our picture taken with him and about a dozen schoolgirls in the background.

We went inside the castle, which was actually a disappointment as the inside was 'modernized' with an elevator and concrete walls. The inside held no appeal in comparison to the exterior of the castle but the view from the top was worth the trip. As we reached the top and stepped out of the elevator, the sun was setting, lending a magnificent pinkish red glow to the sky.

When it was time for Bill's parents to leave we both felt loneliness descend over us and I had to remind myself that we had each other for company. His sister, on the other hand, was entirely alone up in Yamato and I wondered how she would cope during her remaining months in Japan. We made arrangements for Laura to visit us over the Christmas holiday and so she could see where we were living and do some local sight-seeing. But as the holidays approached we were disappointed to learn that we would be assigned classes on Christmas Day. Bill and I were asked to teach a beginner and intermediate class at Kansai Electric Company. This was very difficult to accept considering that every year at Christmas throughout my life I had been surrounded by family, food and gifts and not only was I deprived of this but I was required to work as well. In the end we attempted to be lighthearted about it as we really had no choice. A couple of weeks before Christmas a large box arrived for us at the school. It was a Christmas package from my Mom. Despite it being heavy and awkward to lug through the subway and get it back to our apartment, I was beyond excited to receive a parcel! I anxiously awaited my stop on the train, thinking wistfully about my family in California, being together eating a nice turkey dinner, having fun and exchanging presents. When I finally got home I sat the box down on the floor and ripped it open. Inside were wrapped presents, cookies and Christmas cake. I was just like a little kid, buzzing around the apartment trying to decide where to put the gifts. I realized I had no patience to wait for Christmas Day because I was beside myself with emotion and excitement from having been isolated from friends and family for so long. Bill sat beside me, grinning like a Cheshire cat.

"Let's open them now," I said. I selected a gift and held it up.

"You just can't wait. You'll spoil it for Christmas," Bill remarked. He looked disapprovingly at me.

I knew deep down he was right but my excitement just increased and I couldn't wait any longer. "Really, Bill. What's the point in waiting? It's not like we are going to celebrate Christmas this year on Christmas Day, not when we have to work," I responded. I looked at the beautifully wrapped packages again and then with great energy I began ripping open the presents.

"I got new shoes!" I cried happily. There was also a thick winter sweater for me and one for Bill as well. I felt so grateful for my Mom in that moment, for her generosity and her thoughtfulness. If she only knew what a boost that package was for our emotional well being. Together we celebrated Christmas early, on the bare floor of our apartment. We hungrily began eating cookies and cake as if it were the most extravagant food in the world. There may not have been a turkey, nor a tree, but there was a lot of Christmas spirit in our hearts that evening.

On the morning of December 25th, we got up early, jumping quickly into the shower to warm our rapidly freezing bodies. We then dressed quickly and left the apartment. It was a very cold day as we made our way through downtown Osaka to the electric company. I tried not to think about what day it was and decided to act like it was just an ordinary day. We had little enthusiasm for our classes and our mood was low-key as we worked our way through the day's lessons. One of my students asked me if I celebrated Christmas.

"Yes, of course. It's a very important holiday for me," I told her. Smiling sadly, I thought about past Christmases with my family gathered together for a turkey dinner.

We were relieved when it was time to pack up and go home. We were both quiet and pensive on the ride home. I believed that our company, Interac, needed to create a new policy where foreign English teachers would not be required to teach on Christmas Day. We were fortunate in that our boss was very compassionate and open to change. The following year, we would be given Christmas Day off with pay.

When December 28th arrived, Laura came to spend a couple of days with us. We showed her our favourite places to eat and shop before then planning a trip to visit a well-known castle in Himeji City, a three hour train ride south of Osaka. It was December 31st, my twenty third birthday. The weather had gotten colder and on the train ride down we each huddled into our jackets trying to stay warm. When we finally arrived in Himeji, we walked a long distance to reach the castle. The castle was referred to as the 'white heron' castle because it resembled a giant white heron about to take flight off of the hillside. As we approached the outer gate I noticed that there seemed to be no one around. Generally, at all tourist sites, there are many Japanese as well as foreign tourists milling around or lining up.

Himeji Castle, December 1989

"Don't tell me it's closed," I mumbled.

Laura pointed ahead of her towards the gate. "There's a sign over there, let's take a look," she said. We followed her over to the gate and as we huddled together we read aloud "Himeji Castle is closed December 31st."

We stood in silence. I had tears in my eyes and Laura looked away in disappointment. We had travelled so far and in such horrible weather for nothing. I felt like we had failed in some way because we had wanted to show Laura some interesting sites in the southern part of Honshu and this was supposed to be the highlight of the tour. In resignation we made our way back toward the train station but this time we decided to spend a bit more money and take the express train back to Osaka. Our plan was to have dinner at Karuta Restaurant, located in the Hilton Hotel. Although Bill and I couldn't really afford it, we figured that today was special as it was my birthday after all and it was New Year's Eve too. Perhaps, we thought, a nice meal would compensate for the earlier part of the day.

After getting to the restaurant and being seated, we ordered dinner and drinks. I was relieved to get off my feet and unwind in the warmth of the restaurant. Bill and Laura began talking about their childhood while ignoring my presence as their emotions began to surface. While they reminisced, I sat staring at the elegant tables with their linen table cloths and fine silverware. My mood was beginning to slip when we were approached by the waiter, who indicated it was time to eat. We had ordered the buffet, which was enormous with salads, beef, smoked salmon and an endless choice of desserts. After filling myself with many helpings from the main courses I sauntered over to the dessert table. It was filled with several styles of cakes in every imaginable flavour. They looked so delicate, almost too beautiful to eat. I wished that we had such delicious cakes at home but they simply did not compare to these. Bill and I took extra care to enjoy this meal because it would leave us nearly broke until our next paycheque, which came monthly.

Following our dessert, I looked over at Bill and Laura.

"I'm ready to go. It's been a long day," I said.

"I'll get the cheque and then we'll be out of here," Bill said. He reached into his pocket and pulled out his wallet.

It had been a wonderful meal but the atmosphere was strained and I just wanted to get home and relax. It was a quiet train ride home and by the time we reached Ryokuchi-koen station we were beyond exhausted. I reminded Laura that we still had a 20 minute walk back to our apartment. We still had not bought bikes as our money was tight, but the walk to and from the station was time consuming and unpleasant in cold weather. We knew that soon we would have to part with some money and get some bikes. Along the way we noticed a small wooden table and chairs dumped on the road side. I remembered again about how gomi is garbage that is often worthwhile goods which are thrown away by Japanese homeowners to make room for new purchases.

"Look at this. It's beautiful!" I reached out and picked up a chair.

Bill literally picked up the entire table and asked Laura to grab a chair.

I was about to ask about the other two chairs when Bill said "I'll come back and get the other two chairs."

We walked home in the cold, loaded down with our new dining set.

"Well, you can't say you didn't get a birthday present!" Bill laughed with amusement. I couldn't help but start laughing in spite of the day it had been.

The New Year is a national holiday in Japan but for Bill and I it came and went without much celebration. With the holidays over, we concentrated on teaching and getting private students which would bring in more money.

The bike I had waited so long for

We finally managed to buy two bicycles which were a godsend. Though they made getting around much easier, I found that trying to navigate at high speeds on crowded roads was hazardous to my health. I was hit by several cars either by my own fault or someone else's. One day I was riding along the highway beside the river on my way home when a truck drove too closely alongside me and caught the side of my bicycle basket. The force propelled me forward and I was dragged for several feet before the driver noticed and stopped. As I gingerly stood up, I looked down at my body to see where I was hurt. I was badly bruised with minor cuts but I had no broken bones. My clothes were ruined, my newly purchased chocolate cake was smeared everywhere and I was left feeling pretty shaken up. In shock, I began screaming and the driver was so frightened that he turned around and ran back into his truck and drove off. As I bent down to gather the remains of the cake and my torn books, I noticed blood running down my legs. Although I could see they were just surface injuries, I was bleeding pretty steadily and feeling lightheaded. The worst part, however, was that my bike was beyond repair. Realizing that I could not ride it home, I just left it where it lay on the side of the road and hobbled the rest of the way home. I felt more concerned over the temporary loss of my transportation than I did about the cuts on my body. It would be a couple of weeks before I could replace it and I loathed the thought of having to walk the distance to and from the station once again.

On another occasion, I was racing Bill home and while I turned to laugh at him after taking the lead I pedalled head first into a car that had stopped at a red light and I literally bounced straight up in the air several feet and landed right back on my seat. Bill was horrified and I was shocked but I appeared to be uninjured. After several such incidents I began to slow down but still I put my life on the line each time I rode my bike.

In our efforts to start a home based business teaching students, we had 15,000 flyers printed up and we used our bicycles to deliver them. We piled the flyers into our bike baskets and spent several hours over several days sliding them into apartment mailboxes. My hands and feet would be frozen numb by the time we finished each evening. Then we would sit by the phone and wait for it to ring. A couple of weeks later the phone finally rang. My hand trembled as I picked up the receiver. I couldn't speak more than a couple of words of Japanese and I really had no idea how this phone communication was going to work.

"Moshi moshi," I said. I paused, feeling nervous. "Hello?"

Finally a female voice emerged at the other end of the phone. "Moshi moshi. Keemoo, Bill-san..." The woman's voice was quiet and nervous. Then there was a flurry of Japanese which I did not understand.

I listened, my mind racing. What the hell was I going to do? I had no idea what to say or do next. Then, realizing I had to respond in some way, I spoke into the phone, talking very slowly, in a clipped and abrupt manner. "Do...you....speak....English?" Oh God this was painful.

61

""Een-glee-shoo...teacher?" the voice replied.

"I am Kim. I am... from Canada," I replied.

"Ah! Canada!" I pulled the receiver away from my ear as the voice was now loud and excited.

I was trying to stay focused on the conversation while anticipating how to respond. "I teach English. I can.....meet you at.....Kobeya Kitchen...coffee shop," I said.

"Ah, ah. Kobeya Kitchen!" The woman's voice spoke with affirmation.

I needed information. "What..is..your...name?" I asked.

"Name? My name is Yasko!" Though she was obviously nervous, her voice was dignified and soft.

"Yasko,..I can meet you at Kobeya Kitchen....tomorrow okay?"

"Kobeya Kitchen coffee shop?"

"Yes. Tomorrow at 9:00 in the morning," I answered. I hoped she understood. I was writing everything down as quickly as I could. I was so excited I could hardly believe this was happening!

"Tomorrow morning...Kobeya Kitchen....nine o'clock..yes," Yasko replied.

I only had about a half dozen Japanese phrases up my sleeve. "Hai. Domo arigato," I responded. Then I hung up the phone. I was exhausted and elated all at once.

Bill had been listening intently as he stood beside me. He looked shocked but hopeful. "You got her to meet with you?" he asked.

"Yes! I'm meeting her tomorrow at nine. I can't believe it! This is great!"

Then I put my pen down and sat thinking for a minute. My first possible private student. We had decided that I would be the first to try to connect with potential Japanese students as they were likely to feel more comfortable with a women than a man in this situation. It seemed to have worked. I knew that Yasko must be excited but perhaps uncertain too. I hoped she wasn't afraid of meeting me the next day. We had discovered that some Japanese people were shy around foreigners and seemed unable to know what to say to them. The interesting thing was, Japanese students received several years of mandatory English lessons during elementary school but mostly in reading and writing. The result was that they usually had a good reading and writing comprehension level but they were not used to having to *speak* English.

The next morning I was up early and ready to meet with Yasko. I sat at the kitchen table going through my textbooks, trying to decide which ones to bring along to show Yasko. Finally I grabbed three of them and bundled up in my coat. I promised Bill that I would return right away and let him know how things went. I raced down the stairs outside our apartment, hopped on my bike and pedalled as fast as I could up the hill toward the station. My cheeks were flushed and I was sweating from the bike ride and from nervousness. I arrived at the train station and after parking my bike I walked into the coffee shop looking nervously around. Although no one immediately approached me, an employee yelled out "Irasshaimase!" as I sat down at a nearby table. When the waiter arrived at my table he greeted me with the standard morning greeting.

"Ohayo gosaimasu," he said. He waited patiently for my order.

"Ohayo gosaimasu. Hot cohee, kudasai," I responded.

I waited barely a moment before my hot coffee was brought to me. As I looked up a young woman came up to me, smiling but visibly nervous.

"Keemoo?" she asked.

"Hai. Yasko?" I stood up and shook her hand. I motioned for her to sit down.

We began, tentatively, a simple conversation but I could see she was extremely nervous.

"Please, dozo, relax," I spoke softly. She seemed to understand and then she giggled.

Although Yasko was clearly interested in learning English, she seemed reluctant to commit to paying the advertised fee and she did not want to come to my apartment. We finally agreed on a modest fee and the lessons were to take place at her apartment. I learned that she was a housewife from Gifu prefecture and that she was 26 years old. Her husband was a stockbroker who had been transferred to Osaka and so she too was new to the city. Yasko was to become a close friend. We were both lonely in Osaka and we welcomed the companionship though there was always a subtle distance between us and I felt her respect for me as her teacher. I wanted, over time, to break through that invisible barrier and become a true friend with no strings attached, no cultural barriers but that would prove to be challenging. Despite the cultural gap, I wanted her to view us as equals rather than treat me as the 'foreign English teacher'.

About a week after my meeting with Yasko I ran into her near Ryokuchi-koen station, close to her apartment. I was on my way home from grocery shopping when I saw her.

"Keemoo!" She was surprised at running into me. Even when excited, Yasko somehow managed to speak with a softness in her voice and her mannerisms were quite traditional in the way of the Japanese housewife. She would look down, her bangs falling in front of her eyes.

"Yasko! Nice to see you!" I said enthusiastically. I got a real thrill out of running into a familiar person in a crowd of people where I knew barely a soul. It almost felt like being at home, a normal and welcoming encounter.

She held out two Gerber daisies wrapped in plastic and tied with a pink ribbon. She extended her arm toward me.

"For you. Happy Birthday," she said. She smiled shyly and looked down again.

I was touched. I looked at the flowers she held out to me. They were absolutely beautiful. They had large pink and yellow petals with black centers. In Japanese fashion, they were simple and yet they had an elegant beauty. I took the flowers and smiled at her.

"Thank you so much Yasko......they're beautiful," I said. We talked for a few minutes more and we agreed to meet at her house for lessons the following Tuesday morning.

After securing my first private student, many more were to follow. Things progressed similarly with each initial contact where I would arrange a personal meeting following each phone call. Most students came to our apartment but a few preferred to learn in their own homes. I found out time and time again that though Japanese people had great writing skills in English, their conversational skills were nearly nonexistent. Pronunciation and vocabulary were weak areas and a general fear of failure made learning slow and awkward. But the time spent with my students was rewarding. I learned many valuable insights into their culture. Their generosity towards teachers in general was sometimes overwhelming. When a student remembered a word or an idiom and correctly used it in future lessons, I felt my sense of achievement in contributing to their language development. Over time, my efforts paid off and by having deeper and thus, more meaningful conversations, I felt I was doing my job properly. I learned to make corrections gently, for their pride was easily injured. By spring time, I was teaching from 7:00 a.m. until sometimes 11:00 p.m. My days passed by in a blur. Despite the crazy hours, I was enjoying my newfound career and I was meeting so many interesting people. My students came from all walks of life and included a ballerina, a nightclub hostess, several housewives and high school students and career women.

~

A few weeks later, I woke up in a daze, slowly forcing myself to sit up. I tried to decipher where I was. Was I dreaming? No, I could certainly feel something poking my leg, and it was chilly. As I became aware of my surroundings, I was startled when I realized I was sitting in some bushes, partly hidden from view. My white sweater was covered in small branches and dirt. I realized that I must have stopped here to rest the night before and then passed out. My God! Anything could have happened to me and I knew how very lucky I was under the circumstances that I had chosen to stop here and rest. I had been unnoticed or else who knows what might have happened to me. I looked up and saw that the sky was beginning to get light and I heard traffic driving by. I shook my head to try and rid it of the fuzziness that was affecting my vision. Where was I? I stood up and realized that I was in the same downtown district of Osaka that I remembered from the previous night and then the memory of it came flooding back.

Bill and I had gone out to a club for the evening to have a couple of drinks and unwind from a long busy week. We didn't go out drinking often. The problem for many foreigners when they went out for a night on the town was that the trains stopped running at 11:00 p.m. and that was generally when things starting picking up and people were reluctant to leave. Our only means of transportation on such an evening was the subway as taxis were prohibitively expensive and they wouldn't always pick us up. People would have to make a choice between leaving before 11:00 p.m. to catch the last train, or stay out all night until 6:00 a.m. when the trains starting running again. On this particular evening, Bill and I were having such a good time that we decided to stay, although I was somewhat concerned about drinking for so many hours. I didn't typically drink a lot and I couldn't handle my alcohol very well compared with most people so I would usually limit myself to two or three drinks at most. By midnight, we had been drinking for several hours already and I was feeling hungry so I ordered a salad from the bar. I had eaten about half of it when I looked down and saw a cigarette butt sitting at the bottom of the salad bowl. I almost threw up. Bill was angry and he wondered if it had been done on purpose. In any case, he called the waiter over and pointed out the cigarette butt. The waiter was quite embarrassed and he came back to the table with a new salad, which I refused to touch. He also brought several bottles of booze to our table and he declared that for the rest of the evening, our alcohol would be free of charge. Bill thought the gesture was great but I was less enthusiastic because by this point I had already had way too much to drink and I was wishing that we had taken the earlier train. As the evening crawled into the wee hours of the morning, we ended up chatting with a young man from Australia whose name was Eric. He was friendly and funny and we shared some laughs and enjoyed a lively conversation with him. I knew I would have to deal with a hangover the next day so at this point I stopped drinking but the damage was already done. I could tell that I had consumed too much alcohol and all I wanted to do was go home and sleep it off. Bill, however, did not want to pay the exorbitant price for a taxi and so he persuaded me to stay by telling me that we could take the train home in about four hours. I became bored and hungry sitting there and so we decided to leave and look for a cafe or restaurant that may be open. Eric wanted to come along for something to eat and we agreed to let him accompany us.

As we hit the streets, it was cold and dark and I had trouble walking block after block in my high heels. Eventually we came upon a small restaurant with lights on inside. We ventured in and we could see a group of foreign bikers sitting around a table with a couple of tough looking Japanese men. The owner of the restaurant stood up to usher us out but one of the foreign bikers waved his hand and we were allowed to stay. I nervously sat down and whispered to Bill that I did not want to eat here at this restaurant. I didn't like the look of those men and we speculated that they were likely a group of bikers involved in some sort of deal with a couple of yakuza members. The men resumed their quiet conversation and Bill and Eric reassured me that they had no interest in us. In the end, we ordered plates of eggs, bacon and toast and our meal passed without incident. We paid our bill and left. As we tried to find our way toward a subway which would take us back to the Midosuji subway line, Eric starting talking about love hotels and he asked Bill whether he wanted to visit one with him. I stopped in my tracks.

"Excuse me? Did you just say *love*....hotels? Clearly Eric could not read the shock on my face in the darkness.

"Yeah, that's right," he answered. I tried to read the expression on his face but he seemed nonchalant and unaware of how his remark had affected me.

"I *am* standing right here you know and I *am* engaged to this man. So, you think I am okay with that then?" I shook my head in disbelief at the rudeness of this man.

"Hey, hey, no harm meant, really," he said quickly. He acted apologetic but I could see he was smirking.

"No harm? What exactly did you mean then? Have another drink, friend, on your own," I said. I turned to Bill. "Look, I'm out of here. This guy is a jerk. I am not walking another step with him around," I stated. I was not going to tolerate that kind of disrespect, no matter how drunk he was.

Bill turned to Eric and told him to knock it off and tried changing the subject. But the more Bill tried to change the subject, the more Eric wanted to talk about his adventures in the bars of Osaka. By now, I was exhausted, freezing cold and I wasn't making any progress in getting Eric to leave us and go on his way. I had not wanted to stay out this late in the first place and now we were lost in the middle of the night with a loser who wouldn't leave us alone. I started walking faster away from the two of them, thinking that Bill would keep up with me and that Eric would get the message to take a hike. I was heading home to bed.

I could hear Bill arguing with Eric as I turned a corner and kept walking. I was determined to find my way home. Before long, I began to get tired and I stopped to rest on a low concrete wall which was surrounded with some shrubs. That was the last thing I remembered before waking up a few hours later.

Now it was early morning rush hour and I felt panicky. I must look like a real mess I thought to myself. My head was pounding and I had no idea where I was. I walked for 2 or 3 blocks until I found some subway stairs. I went down the stairs and found a washroom down below. Weakly, I tried my best to rinse the dirt off my face and sweater and shake the loose bits of twigs from my hair. I stared at my reflection in the mirror and I couldn't believe how horrible my appearance was. How did I get myself into this situation? I left the washroom and made my way to the north platform. Somehow I made it to Namba, where I transferred to the Midosuji train and headed home. When I got off at Ryokuchi-koen I felt a huge sense of relief. I found my bike and rode home as fast as I could. When I got in the door of the apartment, I immediately jumped into the shower and then I crawled into my futon, falling asleep instantly.

It was about an hour later when the phone rang. I rolled over, sat up and picked up the receiver. I wasn't feeling very good.

"Moshi moshi," I mumbled into the phone.

"Thank God! I have been out all night looking for you! The police and I have been searching all over Osaka!" Bill sounded very upset.

"What? The police?" I didn't understand.

"Kim, I couldn't find you. I looked up and you were *gone*. We were in a bad part of town. You should *not* have left my side! I thought you had been abducted. Just stay there and I'm coming home!" He hung up the phone before I could answer and I went right back to sleep.

When Bill finally made it back to the apartment, I could see that he was relieved that I was safe. I, on the other hand, was still feeling annoyed at his poor judgment in wanting to stay out all night long. We talked about how I had wanted to go home earlier and that he didn't, nor did he want to pay for a taxi to take us home. The end result of the evening was that I could have been hurt. We agreed that we would never again stay out all night. If we were going to go to a club, either we would leave at 11:00 p.m. or pay for a taxi to get us home.

As a result of this experience, I never drank that much again. I was very careful about how much I drank, where I chose to drink and who I was drinking with. I knew that I was lucky to have made my way back home safely.

CHAPTER 5

Tea Ceremonies, Cherry Blossoms and an Ambulance Ride

In late February, Hirano, a student of Bill's who was a lawyer, invited us to a traditional Japanese tea ceremony at his family home in Nishinomiya, a district near Kyoto. He picked us up in his car and we drove to the neighbouring city. I was excited at the prospect of participating in a traditional ceremony. As we pulled up in front of the house, I looked on in curiosity and admiration. From the street, there was little to see but I could make out the roof line from behind the wall. We were met at the gate by Hirano's elderly grandmother who then ushered us inside. Hirano's parents' home was large by Japanese standards, with a lovely walled garden surrounding it. Inside, the rooms were traditionally decorated with tatami mats and rice-papered doors. Elegantly arranged flowers were placed throughout the home. We removed our shoes while Hirano's grandmother disappeared into an adjoining room. We were told to follow her and as we walked into the room we observed her as she sat on her knees at the back of the room, wearing a beautiful kimono. She smiled and indicated with a tap on her knees for us to join her on the floor and to sit on our knees. In traditional fashion, she expertly crushed the tea leaves in earthenware cups with her head bowed. After waiting patiently for nearly thirty minutes, I was becoming very thirsty. I had never tasted Japanese green tea before but I was willing to give it a try and despite the light greenish colour I took one sip and barely restrained myself from spitting it right out. It was very bitter and salty tasting and certainly not thirst quenching. I glanced over at Bill, who was sitting quietly, shifting his body weight every so often. I was also getting uncomfortable sitting in this manner and wondered how the Japanese were able to sit for so long on the floor.

While I didn't particularly care for the tea itself, I did appreciate the effort that his grandmother went to in serving us traditional tea. I politely finished drinking, holding the cup with both of my hands wrapped around it. His grandmother explained to us that the proper manner was to hold your cup in both hands while drinking and place the cup down on the mat when finished. After the ceremony ended, we retreated to the living room where coffee and cake were served. Despite the language barrier, the family was warm and friendly and it was a very pleasant visit. On the drive home, I reflected how things were looking up for us. We finally had money for food, our social network was expanding and the weather was getting better. I felt optimistic that not only would we survive here but we may even thrive as well, that our life here could be fun if we chose it to be.

Springtime in Japan is a beautiful time of year when the temperature is mild, with endless sunny days and the famous cherry blossoms, known as *sakura,* come to life in April and May. Biking home every day after work I could smell the freshness in the air and I was always so grateful for the tolerable temperature. No more frost-bitten wind and it was not yet time for the sweltering days of summer. Everything seemed to be alive, fresh and happy. People seemed calmer and friendlier at this time of year.

Bill and I had bought tennis rackets months before at a local department store and after our previous experience with attempts at playing some games and then giving it up, we decided to try playing once more. We were eager to spend time outdoors and enjoy the seasonal weather. We began biking to the park for practice sessions on the weekends. Ryokuchi-koen was a haven for city dwellers who would fill up every square inch of the park during nice weather. It really was a beautiful place and many people from all areas of Osaka visited each day to relax and enjoy the surroundings. Just like the previous time, however, I felt uncomfortable as many people would openly stare at us as though we were circus animals and over time this began to wear me down psychologically and physically. Everywhere I went, people would point, laugh or talk about me like I was an object and not a human being. Partly this was cultural behaviour and partly this was me simply being a foreigner. Nonetheless, it was discomfiting to know that every time I stepped outside our apartment people would notice. On the trains, men would reach out and grab me and women would stare and discuss my features as though I were an alien. I found this behaviour unpleasant and it left me feeling constantly harassed. I could not adjust to this difference between eastern and western cultures. Back home in Canada, men would hold doors open for women and allow women to enter elevators first. This chivalrous custom and others like it was a fact of life at home and yet here it seemed the tables were turned. In Japan, women put men on a pedestal. I struggled to accept the overt chauvinism. Of course I realized that not all Japanese men behaved this way but it seemed like a good percentage of them believed that male supremacy was entirely acceptable. These experiences kept piling up daily and weekly until I felt that I had no escape from being watched or touched and so I began to spend longer periods of time inside the apartment.

On one occasion, as I was bicycling home, a car pulled up alongside me and the driver tried to speak to me in Japanese, switching to broken English. He was drunk and hostile looking, veering the car from left to right as he followed me down the narrow road. I gave him the universal salute as I continued pedalling down the road. This encounter was frightening and disturbing as I knew that I was known for miles around as the 'gaijin' or "Canadian sensei" and it was sometimes hard to know when I was being followed home. There were very few people who were unaware of our presence in the neighbourhood and while most were friendly, some were not. The proximity of this incident to our apartment alarmed me the most and it seemed to me that this man knew I lived there and had been waiting.

It was around this time that my weight plummeted to 98 pounds, frighteningly skinny. I normally weighed about 117 pounds and 20 pounds off my petite frame was significant. My hands and lips were constantly blue in colour and my face was emaciated looking. I was scared. I had never given a second thought to dieting or weight as I had been naturally thin my whole life despite a healthy appetite. I then began having chest pains that worsened over time and I thought that maybe my heart was strained from the stress and loss of weight. I made several visits to doctors and hospitals in a vain attempt to find a doctor who could speak

English and who could then find out what was wrong with me. Once, I had gone on my own to a local hospital for tests and after undergoing an EKG test the doctor prescribed nitro-glycerin for me. Common sense and instinct kicked in as I walked out of the hospital that day, holding up the vial to inspect its contents. I was intrigued but a little frightened by the look of it. I was about to take the medicine when I thought better of it and tucked it away in my purse. I found out years later that it would possibly have killed me on the spot had I taken the drug.

On the way to work one afternoon in late spring, I had just arrived at the train station when I keeled over in pain. My chest felt like it was going to explode and my arms had gone numb and tingly. I felt dizzy and weak. I thought for a moment that I was having a heart attack. I found a phone, pulled out my calling card and managed to reach Masa at the office.

"Masa, it's Kim. I...I'm sick, my chest hurts. I can't teach my class today. Please... cancel it for me...I think I need a doctor," I explained. My breathing was quick and shallow. I was unable to take any deep breaths because the pain was too severe.

Masa's voice was full of concern. "Kim, are you alright?"

"I need a doctor. My chest is hurting really bad and I'm dizzy," I answered. I spoke with difficulty, trying to breathe. I had never known such pain and never in the chest area.

Masa quickly arranged for me to see the same doctor who saw me for my kidney infection. When my appointment came the next day I took a taxi to his office. Dr. Ito was there, exactly as I remembered him. He was an astute man, exceptionally kind and wise. He prescribed valium, telling me that I was suffering from acute stress. I thanked him kindly and felt flooded with relief as I left his office and made my way home.

I began taking the valium and things began to improve. Before long, however, my body was weakening and showing further signs of stress. I tried to keep my mind positive, and some things had improved. We now had bicycles and a heater! I was slowly learning Japanese, which I felt was critical for my survival by being able to interact with the Japanese people on a deeper, more personal level. We were earning decent salaries and we had received a good raise as well. In spite of all this, I knew I needed an opportunity to recuperate from the stress of my experience in living in a foreign country without family nearby all while working around the clock. At the end of April, I began to make plans to travel alone to California where my family had relocated to from Virginia.

It was later one morning, close to the end of the month when the phone rang. I had already returned from teaching my early morning class at Shiseido Cosmetics. I now wondered if the school had a cancellation for that night's class, which happened on occasion.

I picked up the receiver. "Moshi moshi," I answered.

"Hello Keemoo," Yasko replied.

"Good morning Yasko. How are you?"

"I am...fine. How are you?" her verbal skills were dramatically improving but still she spoke with hesitation.

"Fine, thank you. What are you doing today?" I asked.

"I clean..my house. But now...I have free time," she said.

"Would you like to visit with me today?" I asked.

"Yes. That would be... good," she answered. She sounded happy at the idea.

We decided to spend the afternoon together and an hour later we met at the train station. It was a cool day but the sky was blue, with only a trace of some silvery clouds. We were going to go to Tokyu Hands department store in Esaka, one station away from Ryokuchi-koen.

We were on the main floor of Tokyu Hands in the stationery department looking at suede diary books. I bought a light brown datebook and then we headed upstairs to the next floor to look around. There was a loft area way in the back of the store that I had not noticed was there before. It held a pet department and so instantly I wanted to take a look. In a cage I saw the most gorgeous looking Persian kitten I had ever laid eyes on. It was pure white, with silver streaks and piercing bright blue eyes. I pointed it out to Yasko.

"Look at this kitten!" I couldn't take my eyes off of it.

"You like...animals?" Yasko asked, smiling.

"Yes, very much," I replied.

"Do you like...to...buy it?" Yasko asked me.

"I don't know. How much is it?" I wondered aloud.

Following behind Yasko, I walked over to the counter. Standing there was a young employee. She was quite young, with long black shiny hair that hung in a straight line down her back. She was immaculately dressed with a white cotton apron over her clothes. Yasko asked the salesgirl how much the cat was. The salesgirl then looked directly at me and replied "..... ju yen". I missed part of the numbers because she spoke so fast. I attempted to clarify the price by again asking Yasko how much the cat was. I finally figured out the amount to be one hundred and forty dollars. It was a lot of money in my mind but I knew I could manage it and I wanted that kitten badly. I looked at Yasko, who was patiently waiting for me to decide what I was going to do.

"Yasko, can you please tell her that I will buy the cat but I must first go to the bank across the street?"

Yasko turned back to the salesgirl and they spoke quietly for a minute. Then Yasko turned to look at me, astonishment in her eyes.

"You must.....really love animals," she said, seriousness in her voice.

We left Tokyu Hands, crossed the street and went into Mitsubishi Bank. I withdrew the money and we went back into the store.

As we approached the pet department, Yasko looked up at me.

"I think you make...fast choice," she said.

I looked at her in surprise. Although Yasko was very honest with me, which was one reason why we got along so well, her words puzzled me. We walked over to the counter and the salesgirl gestured for us to take a seat. There, waiting in the cage, was my beautiful kitten. She had been washed and groomed and she was wearing a pink ribbon around her neck. I felt a surge of joy run through me as I looked at her. I put the money on the counter and waited expectantly for the salesgirl to count it out. The salesgirl picked up the money then looked at me in confusion. She flicked her hair behind her head in a gesture of what I read as annoyance. I wasn't sure what the problem was and I began to feel uneasy. I was sure I had withdrawn the correct amount of money. The salesgirl began speaking rapidly. I glanced at Yasko, who appeared flustered and unable to speak.

"What? What's wrong?" I asked her.

"You need....more.....more money," Yasko said. As she spoke, she cast her eyes downward. I noticed her cheeks were flushed. I was beginning to get upset.

"But you said it cost one hundred and forty dollars," I responded.

"No. It is one....thousand....." her voice was cut off by my bewildered gasp.

"You mean one *thousand* and forty dollars?" I was astounded.

"Yes," she said quietly.

I couldn't believe it. There was no way I was going to pay a thousand dollars for a cat. I stood quietly, looking away, trying to sort through my thoughts. I was feeling extremely embarrassed. I just wanted to leave as fast as I possibly could.

"Please say no. I don't want the cat," I said finally. I looked anxiously at Yasko and then at the salesgirls. There were now two of them, standing there, waiting expectantly. Yasko spoke to them quickly and I watched while they picked up the cat and returned her to her cage. I felt miserable as we left the store. Not only was I embarrassed, but my heart was already attached to that cat. We rode the train back to our station and I apologized to Yasko on the way.

"I'm so sorry Yasko. I didn't understand the amount. I thought it was only a *hundred* dollars," I explained to her.

"No. It is my mistake," she said.

We parted ways and I hopped on my bike and headed down the side streets toward the apartment. The wind was blowing strong as I rode along the highway, struggling to keep my bike upright. I nearly knocked over two schoolgirls walking home from school. I glanced at their matching navy blue uniforms with their crisp white shirts and black backpacks. They giggled loudly, hands over their mouths, astonished to see a gaijin riding past them in a flurry, my blonde hair waving wildly in the wind. What a sight I must be to them I thought! I turned the corner, leaving the schoolgirls behind me as I neared the highway. I then got off my bike and began to walk. There was a long paved path that ran parallel to the freeway, with a river flowing between the two. It was green and quiet along this road and there were several cherry blossom trees lining the edge of the path. I looked at the blanket of pink blossoms beneath my feet. My legs felt cold and I wished that I could get home quicker. I crossed the bridge and got on my bike again for the short ride back to the apartment.

Bill was not at home and I guessed he was probably playing pachinko. It was his favourite way to spend an afternoon. Pachinko was a gambling game involving skill and strategy. Bill would shock onlookers as he won game after game. Japanese men were amazed at his luck and his ability to play. Pachinko machines essentially look like pinball machines standing upright, with little silver balls that are propelled downward by the turn of a dial. The game is played individually with the gambler sitting down in front of the pachinko machine. Bill was getting so good at it that he frequently won about CDN$1500.00 per month.

The apartment was dark. I had covered the kitchen window with airmail paper for privacy. I had not wanted to install blinds as the window was encased with wood and I was afraid of ruining the window casing. The result was that the window did not let in any natural light. I figured it was a matter of privacy versus light and privacy won. I sat at the table and played my Phil Collins tape on the radio. My favourite song, "Paradise" began playing and as my mind wandered over the events of that day I started feeling depressed. I stared at the hardwood floors and the white tile above the kitchen sink as tears were rolling down my cheeks. I cried until I couldn't cry anymore and the collar of my blazer was soaking wet. My mood was black and I remained sitting there at the table for a long, long time. I continued thinking about my loneliness and I was wishing that I could go home to Canada. Then I remembered my upcoming trip to California and I began to feel calmer. As I glanced at the clock on the counter I thought about the upcoming class that I had to teach that evening and I knew I didn't feel like going. I was feeling miserable and so I brought out my diary and began to write. Often, writing was a great release for my pent up emotions. It was a healthy way to vent and sometimes I could work out my problems simply by expressing my feelings on paper. After a few minutes, I stopped, the words and emotions drying up into nothingness. My writing, I could see, was deeply negative. Looking down at the words on the page I realized what a fragile state of mind I was in. Allowing myself this moment to wallow in self pity, I eventually summoned the mental strength to get myself up. Life carries you along and I had work to do. People were expecting me to arrive fresh faced and energetic. I then shut the diary and got ready for work.

I figured I would be able to eat at some point later on and then I organized my lesson plan and searched for my textbook.

I left the apartment, feeling lonely and sad as I once again rode my bicycle to the train station.

~

With the cherry blossom trees in full bloom now, many companies were celebrating this event with their annual *hanami* or cherry blossom picnics. It was a popular tradition for people to gather together to spend an afternoon viewing the cherry blossoms and eating and drinking. One of the companies that I taught for, Shiseido Cosmetics, invited me to their picnic. The party was to take place across the street from the company buildings at a park owned by Shiseido. It was to be held in the afternoon and instead of teaching my regular class I was invited to socialize with the employees and speak English with them.

I arrived on time and as I entered the park, a student of mine, Teruhiko, saw me and came over to greet me.

"Kon-ichi-wa," he said.

"Good afternoon Teruhiko," I answered. I looked at the people scattered around the park.

As we walked toward a large blanket spread out on the grass he asked me "Do you like the ...sakura......cherry blossom tree?"

"They're beautiful," I said as I nodded in agreement.

"In Japan, we have the most beautiful cherry blossom time. We like to view it because it does not last long and then the blossoms are gone," Teruhiko told me. He related a story of an ancient samurai warrior who died beneath a cherry tree. Both the warrior and the blossoms of the tree are admired but they do not live long. I thought about the similarly beautiful cherry blossoms at home in Canada.

"In Canada, we have cherry blossoms too," I said, thinking he might like to know something about Canada.

Teruhiko didn't respond, having already joined his co-workers on the blanket. I watched as they began talking and laughing, wishing I had learned more Japanese. I understood that my role here today was to provide the workers with the opportunity to speak English to a foreigner whose native tongue was English. I was being paid to be here, and to engage the group with idle conversation so that they might practice their conversation skills, building on their vocabulary and pronunciation. Despite knowing this, it felt so awkward to be in such a serene setting with the aim of socializing, yet I was once again an outsider. I looked out at the surrounding canopy of delicate pink and white blossoms and thought what a stunning sight it was. I turned to Teruhiko as he pointed up at the nearest tree.

"This is a most wonderful time of year. Do you enjoy today?" He struggled with his words and I encouraged him by smiling and listening patiently.

"It's amazing, absolutely beautiful. How do you say it - kawaii? Mind you, it is a little cold outside still......" I shivered involuntarily as I keenly felt the chill settling into my bones. Within the next hour, more and more people came trickling out of the buildings, setting up their blankets and trying to find vacant spots.

Teruhiko leaned towards me. "The cherry blossom is very beautiful. But, it is only to view, and not for touching. How do you say........." he was searching for the right word.

"Delicate?" I offered.

"Yes! That is right. The sakura is very delicate flower. But very beautiful. It will only live for one or two weeks. That is why we sit here every year to watch this beautiful sight," he said. He smiled with deep and obvious pride at the blossoming trees before him.

As the hour passed and the air cooled, I politely thanked him. Walking back to the train station, I thought about how symbolic and stunning the cherry blossom was. A short life, but one that was noticed and held in high regard. The flowers bloomed, holding onto the branches as long as possible, before finally letting go and falling off, leaving a carpet of soft petals beneath the tree. It seemed to me that the Japanese aesthetic was about engaging all of the senses, requiring the observer to simply enjoy the scene, without directly impacting the environment. I found this way of thinking and creating to be a disciplined yet peaceful art form.

~

There is a bridge in Osaka called Dotombori bridge. It is commonly referred to as 'lover's bridge' where couples go to meet each other and where single people go in the hopes of finding a lover. One of our students had told Bill and I about this bridge and one day we decided to go find it for something to do. As we stood against the concrete railing looking down into the water of the Yodogawa river Bill held up his eagle pendant that I had bought for him for Christmas before leaving Canada.

"Do you remember when you bought this for me?"

"Of course I do," I said.

"I was really surprised. It was a nice gift," Bill said.

We walked slowly over the bridge to the other side, weaving around several couples along the way. It was surprisingly quiet and peaceful here, right at the center of the city. A brisk wind picked up and I shivered.

"Let's go find something to eat," I suggested.

"How about some ramen noodle soup?" Bill loved the traditional Japanese dishes and although I still preferred food back home I was gradually developing a taste for Japanese food. We wandered down a few streets until we found a small noodle shop. Bill and I ducked under the opening and entered the restaurant. It was very small and crowded inside but we managed to find two empty seats at the counter. When our food was served, we blew on the steaming hot broth and then warmed ourselves up with the hot soup. I looked around at the other diners as they hunched over their bowls, slurping their soup down loudly, a gesture indicating that they found the food tasty. At that moment, I felt relaxed and happy, almost like I was beginning to get the hang of living here and adapting to the culture. After we finished our meal, we strolled past a cake shop and I couldn't help myself from buying an exquisite slice of mousse cake with a fresh raspberry on top. I marvelled at the skill with which food was presented and displayed, it was almost as satisfying to observe the food in the display cases as it was to eat it. We headed to the subway station for the train ride home.

Looking out of the train window, Bill grabbed my knee. "I'll race you home from the station."

"You're on. This time, I'm gonna win!" I smiled, trying to plot how I would out ride him on my bike. It was great fun competing with each other although Bill usually beat me by several minutes.

The announcement came on overhead "Ryokuchi-koen....." as I leaped out the door first in a mad dash to the bike rack. It was always a bit of a game trying to locate our bikes amid the massive pile but mine was a distinct blue and as soon as I spotted it, I jumped on and was off.

Without looking back, I pedalled hard and was soon flying down the hill toward home.

Not long after our visit to Dotombori bridge, I awoke around midnight one evening with severe abdominal pain. It was worse than the chest pain I had experienced. I lay on the futon, trying to sleep and hoped the pain would subside in time. But it did not, it only got worse. Knowing something was seriously wrong I begged Bill to call an ambulance. After many agonizing moments Bill was able to give our address and explain the emergency. I prayed that whoever was on the other end of the line understood enough English so that they would be able to find us. We waited for about half an hour, with Bill sitting beside me as I struggled to cope with the pain surging through my abdomen. The pain never let up. Finally the ambulance arrived and I was carried outside as the neighbours peered out of their windows wondering what had happened.

We drove for a few minutes and then we arrived at a run-down looking building which I found out later was Toyonaka City Hospital.

Inside, the walls were painted a dingy grey colour and the paint was literally chipped and peeling. There were water stains on the ceiling and I was covered with rough looking army blankets.

"Dear God, don't let me stay here," I said as I looked at Bill for reassurance.

Several doctors were called to take a look at me but none could speak English. I lay there in pain, shaking from shock, with tears in my eyes, wondering how things could have gone so wrong. Eventually the doctors decided to take me to Kansai District Hospital, near Kyoto. They explained in simple terms that there was a doctor on duty there who spoke English. I could see the look of concern on their faces and I wished I could speak fluent Japanese so that I could communicate with them. I knew they were trying their best under the circumstances. I was loaded into the ambulance once again and we began the journey that took us through the city. I could feel every twist and turn the ambulance made, trying hard not to move. It seemed every jolt or bump in the road caused shooting pain. My insides felt as though they were burning. This was a new pain, something I had not felt before. The drive was interminably long. I lay in the back of the vehicle, listening to the tinny sound of the siren as it blared on and on. I kept shivering, trying to pull the blanket up higher, trying to get warm. Part of my mind was concentrating on the pain while the other part was thinking what a bizarre and frightening experience this was turning out to be. Roughly an hour and a half later, we arrived at the hospital. It was situated quite far out of the city, up on a small hill. I thought cynically that if I was having a heart attack I surely would have been dead by now.

If I had known what would occur during the next twenty four hours I would have crawled off of that stretcher the moment we arrived at Kansai Hospital. I was in such a state of shock by that point. It was now the middle of the night and I looked up into the doctor's face. I quickly realized that the 'English' speaking doctor *could not* actually speak English , but he did have about five words of French in his repertoire. He immediately removed a black felt pen from his pocket, picked up my arm and drew a large "X" on the inside of my forearm. Without hesitating, he stuck a needle in and injected something which made me cry out from the burning sensation.

"Voila. C'est bien. Allergy test," the doctor announced. He tried to explain in a combination of French and Japanese what he was doing to me. He seemed unconcerned. I was then wheeled out of the emergency area and taken to a room upstairs. I spent the next few hours until morning with Bill hovering over me, both of us afraid.

In the early morning hours I was wheeled into an examining room where a different, younger doctor was waiting to see me. He declared to Bill and I, in perfect English, that I required an emergency appendectomy. Horrified, I searched Bill's face for help. I swung my head from Bill to the doctor, back and forth, my mind trying to comprehend the complete insanity of what was happening to me.

"Bill, listen to me...I know that's not what's wrong," I pleaded desperately. I then asked for a phone and I placed a collect call to my mom in California. The second I heard her voice on the line I broke down from fear and exhaustion.

"Mom, it's Kim.... " I choked on my sobs. "I'm in a hospital, somewhere near Kyoto. I had stomach pain and now they want to operate on me. But I know....that is not the problem," I said. I began to cry uncontrollably as I hung on to the receiver.

"Kim! There's nothing I can do from halfway around the world. I wish I was there with you but I'm not," she answered. I could sense my mother's worry and concern.

"You must be strong, use your instincts, okay?" Her voice changed and she became firm, almost staccato. "You *must* find your strength and help yourself if you are going to make it through this," she said firmly. She paused and I could hear her breathing on the other end of the line.

"Let me speak to Bill for a moment," she demanded. I passed the receiver to Bill, anxiously hanging on to every word he spoke.

This was a scary moment. I could feel my heart pounding, my fear escalating, needing my fiancé and my mother to help me, but I was not going to consent for even a second to having a surgical procedure that I just knew I did not need. Clearly, my mom was as distressed as I was. I knew this was just as hard on her as it was on me, but I also knew that in the end I was on my own and I had to keep my wits about me in order to get through this in one piece. Even though I was scared, my spirit was renewed after hearing my mom's voice.

I told the doctor that I refused to have the surgery and so further tests were ordered. I was then wheeled into another examining room where I had my fourth blood test in less than 24 hours.

"Why are you giving me so many blood tests?" I asked the doctor.

"Here, in Japan, we do things differently," he answered without further explanation.

Shortly afterwards I was placed on a table with my legs in stirrups. Unknowingly, I was about to receive an internal biopsy without any anaesthesia. As the procedure began I screamed out in terror at the searing pain in my lower abdomen. My reflexes were quick and I unintentionally kicked out with my left leg, striking the nurse on my left. She dropped the instruments she had been holding in her hand and there was a loud noise as they landed on the floor. I looked to my right and saw another nurse holding on to a large syringe, with a test tube attached to the end. I watched in complete shock and disbelief as the tube slowly filled up with blood. There was an intense pressure and a burning pain cascading through my abdomen. I had no idea what they were doing to me but I had had enough. Whatever this 'test' was, it was barbaric and would never have happened at home without prior consultation and certainly not without some kind of anaesthetic.

After the procedure was complete I was wheeled back to my room and placed on an I.V. drip without a pole. I lay helplessly on the bed, drained of strength. Although the initial pain had by now subsided, my abdomen was tender and sore. Bill left the hospital to go get some money to pay the hospital bill.. I asked a nurse if I could speak with the doctor. He came into my room shortly after.

"I want to leave the hospital. Please, take out my I.V. I want to go. I know you've done everything you can. Please......" My voice trailed off as I looked at him to gauge his reaction. He moved closer to me and sat down on the edge of the bed.

"You are very sick. You need to stay in the hospital. We will find out what the medical problem is," he answered. He would not remove the I.V.

I stared at his back as he left the room. I wondered what to do next. I continued to ask the nurses in vain to remove the needle but they too refused. When Bill returned a while later I begged him to help me leave. He left the room to speak to the doctor. I learned later that the doctor told him that if I left the hospital now, I would die. There are moments in life like this where events can take a crazy turn without warning. I knew on an instinctive level that I was very ill, but I also felt deep down that I was not dying. This was certain to me, and although I felt this with clarity, I am sure my frail physical appearance must have been alarming to others. With Bill out of the room for a moment, I decided to remove the I.V. on my own, as I knew at this point that no one was going to listen to me. It seemed that, in Japan, doctors had the final say over their patients, while in North America it was the opposite. As a patient, you had to be consulted first, and ultimately you were responsible for deciding to agree or disagree to any surgery or treatment plan. I looked down at the needle. Holding my breath, and pinching the stint between two fingers, I silently counted to three and swiftly pulled the needle out of my arm. I used the gauze that was covering the I.V. needle to press down on my arm to stop the bleeding. It worked! Slowly I began to dress. I was amazed at how weak I was. When Bill came back into the room he stopped dead in his tracks.

"What are you doing? You can't leave!" he cried.

I'm getting out of here and I will get help elsewhere," I said. Ignoring his protests I continued getting dressed. Bill tried to physically hold me down as I struggled to put my shoes on. His face was twisted with agony and fear.

I looked squarely at him and with complete determination in my voice I said to him "I am leaving the hospital Bill. My instinct is telling me to get out of here. I've got to call the embassy and get help. I know my body is sick but if I stay here........I will die," I told him.

Bill released his hold on me and he leaned back against the wall as I finished putting my shoes on. He began to sob, believing the doctor's words that I was going to die if I left the hospital.

I put my good arm on his shoulder. "Bill, listen. It's going to be okay. I just need to find an American doctor who will help me," I said. I was convinced that all I needed was a doctor with a good command of English and an education from an American university and I would then be fine. I felt so bad for Bill as these past couple of days had been hard for him too. He was also worn down emotionally. I knew how much he loved me and I loved him equally. I felt like I was the caregiver at this moment, trying to calm him and reassure him that I would survive.

We left the hospital against the doctor's orders. We walked very slowly to the nearest train station. By now, I was very weak. I struggled to take in my surroundings but I was with it enough to notice the quiet grey of the sky and people standing beside us waiting for the train to arrive.

When we eventually got back home, I immediately called the Canadian embassy. The Consulate General was on the line within seconds. He gave me the phone number of his personal doctor in Kobe City, an hour away. I contacted the doctor, a British national who had studied at Oxford University. I made the appointment for that same day. Bill and I made our way to the train station and arrived at the doctor's office 2 hours later.

The doctor's office was about 3 blocks from the train station and I struggled to walk those blocks which took us up a steep hill. My breathing was laboured and my muscles were not strong enough to carry me that far. I had to frequently stop to catch my breath, and I worried about being late for my appointment. Finally we made it up the hill and as we entered the small waiting area I glanced around at the patients waiting quietly. There were three men in the waiting room, all dirty looking, possibly navy men. They looked dishevelled and drunk. I wondered what kind of clinic this was. I explained to the receptionist about my call earlier and gave her my name. I was asked to have a seat and I held tightly onto Bill's hand as I nervously waited to be seen. When I finally got to see the doctor my first impression was that he was gentle and capable. I was immediately reassured and I felt all my fears melt away as he spoke to me and asked me about what had been happening.

"Tell me about your health in general," he said.

I briefly told him of my kidney infection and previous problems coping with stress since I had been living in Japan. He seemed sincere in wanting to know about my overall wellness, or lack of it. I sighed heavily, leaned back against the chair and thought back to all of the pain and problems I had been having. As he listened, he nodded his head silently.

"We'll just do a quick blood test...it won't take long. Just relax," he said. He produced a syringe and as he drew my blood I watched quietly. He then stepped out of the room and returned moments later.

"You do have a low white blood cell count, and your body's immune system does appear weak but there is no obvious sign of infection or disease. I suspect your inner chest cavity is inflamed, causing those sharp pains you've been having. This pain, which can be severe, can radiate down to the lower abdomen. I believe you have an inflammation of the muscles in the chest cavity." He handed me a packet of pills in a small white paper bag.

"Take these muscle relaxers when you feel you need to," he told me. He stood up and shook my hand.

"You'll be fine. But you're going to have to find a way to reduce your stress. It's not good for you. I know Japan can be stressful," he said. He smiled sympathetically.

I stood up, thinking how quick and easy that was. It was so simply diagnosed. All these months of pain in different regions of my body and it's remedied in 10 minutes with a bag of pills?

"I want to thank you. It's been tough, but I'm sure I'll pull through," I said as relief flooded through me.

"How long do you plan on staying in Japan?" he asked.

"I don't really know for sure. We signed another one year contract. We kind of take it year to year," I replied.

"You may want to consider taking a holiday, getting away from Japan for awhile," he said.

"I am planning to do that," I answered.

"Well, take care of yourself. It was nice meeting you," he responded and then he walked out of the room.

I met Bill in the waiting area and we left together, walking back to the central train station. As we rode the train back toward Osaka, I thought about everything that had happened. I was a little hesitant to really believe my problems could be over so quickly.

I took my pills regularly over the next few weeks and I started to feel more relaxed again. My health improved steadily as I looked ahead to my trip to California. I would continue to struggle with the difficulties of living as a foreigner in Japan, but my emotions would never again be as low as they were that spring. I thought again of the cherry blossom trees with their delicate pink petals that fell softly to the ground. Usually a final strong wind would clear the branches clean of the remaining petals. I felt that, like the cherry blossoms, I would come alive again. I only hoped that it would not be short lived.

CHAPTER 6

Lake Bhiwa

The first week of July came swiftly and I prepared to leave for California. Bill was naturally sad to see me go and leaving him behind after all we had been through together was very difficult. Although I had recovered physically, I was still emotionally fragile and I longed to leave Japan for awhile. I was extremely excited at the idea of seeing my family again after almost a year. I couldn't believe so much time had passed since we had seen each other. As I hugged and kissed Bill goodbye at the airport and boarded the plane, I thought how the last time I had seen my family was at the airport in Vancouver. It was now 1990, a new decade had begun and I had changed so much! I knew they would be shocked by my appearance. I was painfully thin, not the girl I used to be. Other changes had occurred as well. I was dressing considerably more stylish, my clothing chosen with care based on the latest Japanese fashions which were right on the heels of the runways of Paris and New York. I was looking good but I was too skinny. I hoped maybe I could gain some weight back in California.

On the 11 hour flight, I drank enormous amounts of orange juice, remembering how my feet had become swollen the last time I flew. As I glanced around the half empty plane I noticed that I was the only woman on board. I was now used to being a novelty, and so this fact did not bother me in and of itself, but I wondered how I would pass the time on this long flight. I wasn't sure I would even be able to engage any of the passengers in conversation or if they would attempt to speak English. It also occurred to me that if the plane crashed, I might not have anyone to talk to in my last moments! The plane, like last time, held mostly Japanese businessmen headed to America for business. Deciding to give it a shot, I turned to the man seated beside me.

"Hi, how are you? Heading to the States for a business trip?" I asked.

He turned to look at me and explained that he was from Osaka, but working in Tokyo. He was on a business trip for a toy company that he worked for. His assignment was to search out new and interesting toys on the market in the U.S. and bring the ideas back to Japan. I was intrigued by his job and because he was fluent in English we were able to carry on our conversation for nearly five hours.

After dinner was served, a passenger behind me removed his socks and somehow stuck his smelly foot through the opening between the seats and he rested his foot on the arm of the chair about an inch from my arm. When the sweaty smell hit my nose, I looked down and pressed my elbow firmly against his foot. The foot wiggled madly for a moment but it stayed put. I sighed heavily. "This is going to be a long, long flight," I thought to myself.

It seemed the travellers were all trying to get in a comfortable position for the last half of the flight. Some of the men were trying to sleep in contorted positions while one I saw had lucked out and found three empty seats together. He had simply spread out across all three seats and gone to sleep. I myself was too excited to sleep and I flipped through magazines and just rested, happy to be heading in the direction that I was.

When we landed in L.A. I was so wound up that I could barely restrain myself from flying down the aisle. After clearing customs, I spotted my parents, Terry and Donna, and my younger brother Ryan. I rushed up to them and grabbed them all in a big hug, shaking and sobbing, relieved to be with them after such a long separation.

It was the first time I had been to their home in L.A. My dad had been transferred to California from Virginia at the same time that Bill and I had left for Japan. They lived in a nice middle class suburb in the San Bernardino valley. They had a large banyan tree growing outside the dining room window and a cactus covered hill for a backyard. The weather was pleasantly warm which was a reprieve from the humid rainy season months back in Japan.

Both my parents were shocked by my appearance although they tried to make me feel relaxed and comfortable. My hair, usually very thick and wavy, had fallen out at the nape of my neck and I was so thin. My moods switched from happy to sad within seconds. I spent a lot of time crying, relieving all the stress and pent up emotions that I had been feeling for many months. Mom took me shopping at nearby boutiques to keep me busy. I was ecstatic at being able to browse the racks and find tons of clothes that fit. Waist size? No problem. Shoes? No problem. I was on cloud nine and spent freely, filling up my suitcase after each shopping trip. My mom introduced me to her neighbours and she showed me the office where she worked.

One day she took me to Laguna Beach, just her and I. We spent the afternoon walking along the shoreline and picking up seaweed. I felt good, I felt free and most importantly, I felt relaxed again. Nobody was staring at me, nobody was giggling and pointing at me. I felt normal once again. That first week flew by very quickly and I was sad to have to leave the sanctuary of their house but they had previously planned a summer getaway to Myrtle Beach in North Carolina and I had no choice but to tag along. The thought of going even further away across the continent and therefore further away from Bill was upsetting to me. I was already missing him so much. He was in my thoughts constantly throughout the day, and though I was happy to be out of Japan for awhile, I wasn't as happy being apart from him. We had grown so close in our relationship and I knew we were meant to be together. The experiences we had had together had deepened our bond and I was grateful to have him in my life.

Myrtle Beach, on the eastern coast of the U.S. alongside the Atlantic Ocean, was a beautiful place. The beaches were wide, with soft pale sand and the water was very warm. Growing up in the northwest on the Pacific side of the continent, I was accustomed to much colder water in the ocean. I marvelled at the homes which were built on stilts and there was a real small town beach atmosphere. People were friendly and outgoing. It was a typical beach community and I started enjoying myself despite the circumstances. We spent our days laying on the beach, soaking up the sun, swimming in the ocean or playing cards at the beach house. On the surface, everything seemed well yet I missed Bill terribly. We had been constant companions in a foreign country where sometimes speaking to each other was the only solid communication we had. I decided after a week in North Carolina to call him in Japan. I phoned collect, my heart beating rapidly in the anticipation of hearing his voice. The phone rang several times and I checked my watch again to calculate the time difference. Japan was nearly a day ahead and I had to call him either early in the morning or later at night if I was going to reach him. The line suddenly clicked on.

"Moshi moshi," Bill's voice came through the line.

"Hi Sweetie!" I said excitedly. I couldn't help smiling. There was a long pause. "Bill?"

"Yeah. How are you?" he answered. He sounded weak.

"I'm fine. We're in Myrtle Beach. I just had to call you.........I miss you so much," I said. I tried not to cry.

"How was your flight?" he asked.

"Hah! Well it was interesting," I answered. I told him about the incident with the man and his foot sticking into my arm.

He laughed. "I'm glad you're relaxed and having a good time. You needed it," he said.

"Hey, are you okay Bill?" I was concerned by the sound of his voice.

"I'm doing a bit better now. I've been pretty sick. A couple of days after you left I woke up with a fever, I've been sick as a dog. I couldn't even get up to eat I was so weak. Then there was no food here and I couldn't make it out to the store for food," he explained. He paused again as he coughed into the phone.

"Oh my God. I'm so sorry. I wish I had been there. I feel so bad that you're alone. Do you have food now? Are you alright?" My heart sank. I felt guilty for leaving him alone but I was also worried about whether he was getting help or able to get food by himself.

"I'm okay. Masa called and asked if I needed anything but I told him I didn't need anything. I miss you. I love you. I can't talk anymore sweetie. I've got to go lay down," he said.

I held back the tears as he coughed again.

"Bill, I hope you're going to be okay. I love you so much," I said. Feeling distraught, I said good-bye and hung up. My stomach constricted and I wanted to leave that moment and fly straight back to Japan to see him. He had me worried. Bill rarely got sick, he had a very strong immune system and I had never seen him bedridden in all the time I had known him. I lay awake all that night, unable to stop thinking about him and wondering if he was okay.

The next two days were hard as I battled my depression once again. I was sliding into a hole, crying all the time. My family kept their distance from me, sensing that I needed space to get myself together and get a handle on my emotions. I had not brought any of my pills with me as I did not think that I would need them anymore. Clearly, they would have helped me to cope but I was going to have to find a way on my own to crawl out of my depression. Over the next several days I continued to phone Bill daily, needing to hear his voice and connect with the one person who could understand what I had been through and who could relate to my 'stories' of daily life in Japan. Bill and I would both discover, upon my return to Japan, that these daily calls would add up to a princely sum of around US$2,000.00!

One evening I woke up from an afternoon nap and found my younger brother Ryan, sitting on the living room couch. He appeared lethargic and he had a deep chest cough.

"Hey Ryan, are you okay?" I looked at the paleness of his face.

He shook his head. I sat down beside him and touched his forehead. He didn't seem too warm. He mumbled something and continued to lay there, trying to breathe. The house we were staying at belonged to Clay and Ann, friends of my parents and they, along with their kids and my parents were still out at the beach. I wandered into the kitchen and stared at the empty beer bottles stacked up on the counter. I opened up the fridge and grabbed a can of Sprite for Ryan. I brought it back to him and he took a couple of sips, gasping for air each time. Ryan had always struggled to breathe in humid climates. He suffered from asthma and humidity often triggered it. I reached over and flicked on the T.V. as Christa, Ann's eldest daughter, came into the house. She was a few years younger than me and still in high school. Perhaps because of my dark mood and the fact that she had brought her boyfriend along, we hadn't really spent any time together. I felt better this evening and I was eager to get out of the house and do something.

"Hey Christa. Are you into playing a game of tennis?" I asked her.

"Yah sure. Let's go get the rackets," she said and turned around and headed back outside.

Leaving Ryan asleep on the couch, I followed Christa outside and we walked down the roughly paved roads, watching as black clouds streaked across the sky. I was worried about lightning as it scared me and I knew storms in North Carolina could be bad. On the east coast, storms could be violent and people here died every year from lightning strikes. We arrived at the tennis courts and we played for about half an hour before Christa started to lose interest. With nothing better to do we headed back to the house. About halfway there the rain started and we laughed as we ran back, hoping to make it to safety before the lightning started.

Back at the house I went into my room and lay down, trying to sleep.

"You gonna sleep your life away?" my dad asked as he leaned his head into the room.

I opened one eye and shrugged.

"Come and help me make dinner," he said as he pointed to the kitchen.

"What are we having?" I asked, only half interested.

"Fresh shrimp," he said.

I stood at the kitchen sink peeling and deveining shrimp. Dad was frying butter, garlic and onions in the pan. I had two huge bowls of peeled shrimp done when the rest of the gang showed up. We sat down to a delicious feast of fresh seafood and beer and we lingered lazily over the meal.

After dinner, I headed back to my room, leaving my parents and their friends to their beer and card game. I was too miserable to party with them. I wanted to be with Bill. I couldn't believe it when I realized I was actually looking forward to returning Japan.

We returned to L.A. the next day and my trip was coming to an end. Mom and Dad's neighbour, Nancy, came over with some cupcakes to say good-bye. It was a very thoughtful gesture. She gave me a big hug.

"Come back and visit us anytime," she said. I believe she really meant it. I was impressed by how friendly people were in California.

We drove to the airport in silence. Ryan seemed upset at my leaving, and it had been good for both of us to spend time together again, playing video games and bonding as siblings should. At the airport my Mom wrapped me in her arms in a big hug.

"I don't want to go back Mom," I said. I was despondent. Leaving my family again was difficult.

"I know. You'll be okay. Bill is waiting for you," she said, smiling at me. She was trying hard to look and sound upbeat and positive.

I hugged my Dad.

"Hey, thanks for having me. I had a good time and it was nice having a break from everything," I told him. I was going to miss him too.

"Anytime sweetheart. You take care of yourself," he said and he kissed me good-bye.

I turned around once and waved at my family as I boarded the plane. From my seat I could see them standing behind the glass window of the terminal, waving and smiling at me. I turned and waved back again.

"Good-bye," I whispered.

~

Flying eastward took only nine hours and the flight went by quickly. As we neared Osaka I felt happy and lighthearted. I was surprised by my own joy at returning to Japan. After disembarking from the plane I eagerly scanned the sea of faces in front of me. Then I saw Bill waving madly at me. I bounced through the line, my slender, deeply tanned legs swinging along. I was wearing a white blazer with matching shorts and my latest fashion statement - my 'Crocodile Dundee' hat. As soon as I passed through the security gate I ran to Bill and jumped into his arms as he wrapped me up in a bear hug. He was grinning nonstop, not taking his eyes off my face. I stared back. It was a funny feeling because he looked so different to me, almost like he was a total stranger. When I told him this he said he felt the same way. We hugged and kissed and grabbed my luggage.

"You look so good!" he beamed at me.

"So do you. But it's strange. It feels funny..... I haven't seen you in five weeks....." I looked up at him and smiled.

"Let's go home," he said. He took my suitcase from me and held me by the hand as we walked towards the Hankyu train station.

We lived fairly close to the airport and we were home within an hour. The strongest feeling I had was that everything looked familiar. The neighbourhood, the apartment, the sounds and smells, all of it I recognized and I realized that I had missed it without knowing it. It felt....good. I was happy to be here with Bill. I couldn't wait to phone Yasko and tell her I was back. But first I had to unpack some gifts I had brought Bill. We sat down at the kitchen table and I recounted my trip for him while giving him his gifts. He was thrilled by the clothes, leather sandals, a new watch and some books to read. As we sat and talked I asked Bill again about his illness. I was shocked when he told me how bad he had really been. For two days he had been flat out on the floor, unable to get up, while he battled a fever and a pounding headache. He told me that the pain through his body was pretty bad and that he sweated continuously. It was on the third day that he forced himself to get up, get dressed and go out to get some food. He brought back some fruit and some yogurt. He had only had water to drink for the first two days and he had been very weak. It scared me to think how sick he had been and that he had been alone with no one to help him. I tried to put the image out of my mind. I was grateful to be with him and to know that he was now healthy and that everything was going to be alright. That night, for the first time in a long time I slept soundly and my life felt complete.

I had a few more days to unwind from jet lag before returning to work. In the meantime, the school had invited all of the instructors to a summer picnic at Lake Bhiwa, near Kyoto. A group of us met on the Hankyu train line and we travelled together. It took several hours on the train before we arrived at our destination station. We were picked up there by one of the company's salesmen who then drove us to the lake. As we assembled together on the beach we had a moment to relax and refresh ourselves before being taken out on a jet boat to the other side of the lake where the other teachers and staff were waiting. When we finally jumped down from the side of the boat and waded through the water we were eager to settle ourselves down and enjoy the day ahead. Tables and coolers of food and drinks had been set up and we had free use of windsurfers and jet skis. It was incredibly well organized.

Lake Bhiwa

The administrators and supervisors of Interac at the Osaka Branch Office were very kind and welcoming to their foreign staff. They were always there to lend support, financially or personally. They never turned their back on someone in need. On the many occasions that I had been ill or had questions their assistance was always forthcoming. Masa, our head supervisor and Taeko, an administrator, were both exceptionally compassionate individuals. I was so grateful for their warmth and caring manner. I was always treated with the utmost respect. I really enjoyed my job and I was satisfied with the company and I felt, for the first time in my life, that I had a career that I was proud of, one that challenged me to continue learning how to be better at it. I saw Mikki, the office secretary, standing near a jet ski and so I wandered over.

"Hello Kim!" she smiled brightly at me and waved.

"Hi Mikki! How are you?" I smiled back at her as I approached.

"Great! And you?"

"I'm doing well, thank you. Glad to be back," I said. I really meant it.

"We are glad to have you back Kim. You must have a good time today and enjoy yourself, okay?" she gestured to the jet skis. "You should go for a ride!"

"I think I will!" I took off my sundress and with my bathing suit on underneath I was ready to go. I picked up a life jacket from the sand and as I put it on, one of the salesmen standing beside me asked if I knew how to operate the jet ski.

"I sure do," I said and walked out into the water and got on the jet ski. I started up the ignition and then I pressed the accelerator. I did fine until I had to make a turn. As I tried to circle around to head back I nearly lost my balance as I was going faster than I had intended. The salesman waved me in and when I reached the shore he jumped on In front, taking over the control of the jet ski. He took the throttle and handles and spun it around in tight circles. I laughed as the water came spraying up in our faces and soaked us. I was enjoying the freedom of being out on the water. We headed back to shore to dry off in the sun. The wind had started to pick up and the waves were getting big. As we came in, I saw Bill waiting at the shore for me.

"You have a good ride?" he asked.

"Yeah awesome, but it's getting pretty windy out there," I said and pointed behind me.

"Pass me your life jacket. I'm gonna take a spin for a minute," Bill said. He reached over as I got off and I handed him my life jacket as he sat down on the jet ski.

I stood watching as Bill bolted straight out into the lake, unafraid of the waves smashing into him. I chatted with Mikki and Taeko as we all kept an eye on Bill out on the lake.

"It is very windy," Taeko said, her hair blowing in her face. She struggled to keep it out of her eyes.

"Yes it is. But it keeps the air cooler," I answered. I looked behind me at the coolers. I was getting thirsty and hungry now.

Bill suddenly zoomed in, taking less care to slow down than I had. We jumped out of his way as he parked it right on the edge of the beach blankets.

"Hey Bill, you're supposed to come in slowly!" I was surprised at his carelessness.

"Hey, no problem. I knew what I was doing," he said and shrugged.

"Let's go get something to drink," I said and we started walking over to the tables.

We jointed the rest of the group as we lay out our bamboo mats we had brought with us. Bill handed me a beer and I greedily began gulping it. It was very windy, and the sky was crystalline blue. Everyone was relaxed and in a happy mood.

Masa looked over at us. "Hard to believe that this water is our drinking water. Do you know, it supplies Kyoto and Osaka residents?" he asked us.

"Really?" I said. I looked out at the lake in disbelief. Drinking water? With hundreds of bodies swimming and jet boats and jet skis cruising through, it seemed hard to believe. As I stared out at the lake, I recalled an afternoon when I decided to run water through my coffee maker to purify it. When I looked in the filter it was full of silvery brown gobs of some unknown substance. From then on I made a point of buying only purified water for my coffee. Nearly every day I would wipe out my nose which would be coated inside with black soot. We were breathing in a lot of pollution all the time. The air quality was particularly bad further south past Namba where there was more heavy industry. I absent-mindedly wiped my nose on my sleeve as I gazed at the black plumes of smoke firing out the back of the boats and the jet skis.

We ate our okonomiyaki pizzas and drank more beer and then I decided to give windsurfing a try. It was something new for me but I was willing to try. Despite my best intentions, it seemed beyond my ability as I would precariously find my balance and then a wave would come in and over I went. Again and again. I laughed along with several observers at my repeated attempts to stay upright.

With the wind blowing hard, we were unaware of the heat and so we were quite comfortable as we lay back and dozed on our mats. When I finally sat up, it was late afternoon, and people were starting to get organized to leave. I rolled up my mat and along with Bill, joined the first group of teachers who were heading back across the lake. Once on the other side, we were again driven back to the station where we all slumped down into our seats, clearly worn out but all of us content.

It was after 11:00 p.m. by the time we finally got back to the apartment. I had felt a little light headed on the way home and I could feel my back stinging as I undressed and got ready for bed. As I lay down on the futon I immediately felt the raw pain of the burn on my skin.

"Bill, I can't lay on my back. It hurts too much," I said. My skin felt tight and sore.

"Tell me about it. Turn around and let me see your back," Bill said. He carefully pulled up my shirt. "Oh my God, you are burnt. I mean really, really burnt. You're entire back is beet red," he said. Gently, he lowered my shirt and I lay there for a moment on my stomach, feeling the heat come out of my skin. I could now feel my thighs stinging. It seemed that I would not be able to get comfortable no matter what position I tried to sleep in. I forced myself to stand up and then I staggered into the bathroom where I ran towels under cold water. I brought the towels into the bedroom and placed them on the futon.

"Okay, let me see your back. Sit up so I can see it," I said. I looked on as Bill sat up, his back facing me. "I have never seen a burn like this before. It might be worse than mine," I told him. I picked up a towel and laid it over his back. Then I grabbed another towel and flipped it over my head onto my own back. We sat there, completely tired out, trying to soothe our skin. Within minutes the towels were bone dry. I continued to wet towels all through the night, trying to draw out the heat from our skin.

By the morning, I was feeling worse. Every time I tried to move my body, my skin would stretch tightly, pain shooting through every nerve ending. I was dehydrated and my face was swollen. I tried to get up but found I was unable to walk. I lay back, helplessly watching as Bill slowly got dressed for work. He gave me a kiss goodbye and he left. I didn't have a class scheduled until the evening and I was thankful to have some extra time to stay home and pray that my skin would start healing. So I spent the entire day applying aloe lotion and damp towels and laying flat on my stomach. At around 4:00 p.m., I forced myself to get ready for work. Every time I tried pulling on pants my legs would burn like crazy from the irritation and so I finally settled on white shorts with a thin blue cotton shirt. I tried but was unable to get my matching blazer on over my burned shoulders so I tossed it back in my closet. I grabbed my hat and my books and left.

My skin was too burned to bend my legs up over the bike so I had to settle on walking but it would add 20 minutes to my travel time to get there. I was no longer used to the long, uphill walk to the station and it took me nearly half an hour to reach the platform at Ryokuchi-koen. I got on the train and sat down, looking at the cars go by on the freeway above. The train always seemed to move faster than the cars. It was busy but not yet rush hour. The mornings were the worst for taking the train. People would be crammed in and nearly every part of the body was touching someone, somewhere. In the summer, the fans that hung from the ceiling would twirl around, trying vainly to cool the air down and ward off the humidity. Bodies would become drenched with sweat and the doors would open at each stop only to let in more people. There were men who worked on the platforms, pushing in bodies at certain main stops during morning rush hour. If you were standing near the door, you could see men in blue uniforms, their white gloved hands moving about as they shoved limbs inside just before the doors slid shut. Their hands would raise toward the driver of the train as the whistle blew for the all clear to start moving down the track.

At last my stop, Yodoyobashi, arrived. I got off the train and headed up the endless stairs and along the walkways. I had some extra time despite my earlier walk and so I went into a coffee shop in the sub-way. I sat down at a little table and ordered coffee and chocolate cake. My skin felt like sandpaper by now and I was wondering how I was going to make it through the rest of the evening. The class I was going to teach was for several businessmen at Nisso Shoji. They were very patriarchal and difficult to teach. I figured that like every other teacher, I had some wonderful students and some who were just fulfilling their boss's request to learn English. I remembered my first night teaching this class and as I entered the room that first time, the female students who worked as secretaries, stood up politely and exclaimed "Kawaii! Pretty!" as I stood uncomfortably at the front of the room. They would generally rush around preparing tea and cleaning ashtrays while the men sat at the tables. I found it strikingly different in Japan with regards to the gender bias, and how women were treated here. At home, though men still earned more on average than women, the gap wasn't as wide as it was here and I had always felt equal to my male co-workers.

I sighed as I entered the building once again and made my way to the conference room. Everyone was in there, waiting patiently for my arrival. When I walked in, there was a collective silence as a dozen pair of eyes focused on my beet red face and legs. I greeted everyone and as usual, opened the class with a few minutes of 'free' conversation.

"How was your trip?" one of them asked.

"Very good. Nice to see my family but I am happy to be back. I hope everyone studied Chapter 7!" I smiled at them as I brought out my tape and placed it in the cassette player. I opened my textbook and asked the students to do the same.

"We're going to start with Chapter 7, Kenji's Office. Let's listen to the tape and then we'll discuss the answers afterwards," I instructed. I hit the play button and sat down in my chair. I listened along with the students *"Kenji has a new office. He will have his own desk. There is a plant next to the window and a picture on the wall. There is a clock on the wall above his desk...."* I watched as the students tilted their heads, trying to catch the words. Some of them were frowning at the speed and the vocabulary on the tape.

"Miss Kim, I can't understand. Please play again," asked Hiroshi as he sat back in his chair and crossed his legs in frustration. One of them said something in Japanese and they all began to laugh. I hit the rewind button and then the play button again as I sighed heavily. I looked at my watch. It was 7:05 p.m. I still had an hour to go I thought, as the tape began to play once more.

*With **my private student Mali and her
mother getting ready for the O-Bon Festival***

Following my busy schedule of travelling and teaching, at the tail-end of summer, I was invited out by one of my private students, Mali, to attend an Obon Festival at the town center of Ryokuchi-koen. The Obon festival is when Japanese families remember their ancestors. Perhaps to make Bill and I feel included, and to encourage us to take part in some of the festivities, Mali and her mother, a ballet studio owner, arrived at my apartment one afternoon to dress me up in a *yukata*, which is basically a summer kimono. I was amazed at the length of time it took them to dress me properly, Mali's mother making sure every part of the cloth was folded correctly. I learned a great deal that afternoon about the precision and patience necessary in order to wear the yukata properly. Mali and her mother were incredibly warm and caring people and I thoroughly enjoyed my time spent with her during our lessons. Mali's English speaking was in fact very fluent but she wanted to take lessons to avoid losing some of her fluency, which can happen when you don't speak a second language very often. After I was properly dressed, we piled into Mali's car and she drove us up to the town centre, where we walked around viewing other women in their yukata's and admiring all of the lanterns strung along the paths. It was a magical evening and a perfect ending to my summer.

CHAPTER 7

Autumn Typhoon

The summer was nearing an end and it had passed without a rainy season which was very unusual. The year before we had seen endless days of torrential downpours. People would scurry about with their matching raincoats and umbrellas as they went about their daily activities. This summer had seen hardly any rain at all.

September began with clear, sunny skies and the air was fresh. One of my favourite things about Osaka were the trees in our neighbourhood, which would bloom in late August and the fragrance from the blooms was like the scent of fresh peaches. Sometimes I would go for walks in the park and just inhale that delicious smell.

Bill's sister, Laura, was leaving Japan and returning to Canada now that her 2 year contract was up. At first I thought how lucky she was to be going home but I began to feel that being in Japan was a great opportunity for us. My attitude had changed dramatically this summer and I was now finding life here easier and more enjoyable. The dark clouds of my depression had lifted and I was in a much better frame of mind. I found that every day I was rediscovering things in Japan that I had previously overlooked or been unable to find pleasure in. The food in Osaka was actually very good and we had by now searched out some excellent restaurants. We were also making more money and this enabled us to eat better and to get out and do a lot more sightseeing. We spent weekends visiting museums, amusement parks and even neighbouring cities. Another factor that we considered was that income tax in Japan was minimal when compared to Canada and here we had the ability to earn more and save more. We had overcome the initial hardships of getting set up in our lives here and in struggling day to day with money. We talked about whether we should leave or stay longer. I frequently asked Bill about our motive for staying longer. We had been here for one year now and clearly our efforts were paying off. We had good jobs and we had several private students as well. We felt comfortable after all that hard work we'd done in the beginning. We knew that the money that we were earning here would be impossible to earn at home unless we were holding down 3 jobs each. Bill was much more concerned about making money than I was. I would have agreed to leave at that moment if he had also agreed but he wanted to stay. So we signed another year long contract. I thought about how quickly this summer had passed and I told myself to enjoy Japan while I had the chance.

~

Fall was quickly arriving and I was busy teaching and focusing on trying to develop more creative lesson plans. I began to bring a video camera to some of my classes and for one particular class I asked the students to form groups and choose a product that they would like to convince the other groups to buy. The students found this approach to learning very different but they quickly warmed to the idea and participated with a great deal of enthusiasm. I asked them to create their dialogue in English and then I would film each group when they were ready. The results were entertaining and we shared laughs while the student's learning curve rose sharply. Now they were motivated. Realizing that I may be on to a good idea I tried using a similar format but I would alter it according to the background and age of my learners. For one class, comprised mainly of young male workers, I asked them to design and 'sell' their fantasy car. It went over extremely well. I was enjoying my work more than ever and I continued to build my student portfolio for private lessons. With all this hard work I was earning more money and I had no problem spending it. I felt that because I had earned it I was entitled to do with it as I chose and Japan was not lacking in consumer goods. I began spending my money on clothes, cosmetics, purses and whatever else I felt like buying. I became obsessed with buying fashion magazines and even though I couldn't read any of the articles I could look through the pictures and get a sense of what was in style. This began a lifelong interest in magazines and fashion. I thought nothing of spending fifty dollars on a tube of Christian Dior lipstick.

I had also met a fellow gaijin at a department store and we shared stories about the challenge of trying to find clothing that fit. She mentioned that I could probably get modeling jobs based on my 'look' and my thin frame. I had never thought about modeling in Japan as a possible job but for a few days I gave it some serious thought. Then finally I picked up the phone and contacted a local agency. I was asked to come in for a meeting that afternoon. Hanging up the phone, I thought how unprepared I was. I really wasn't sure if this was what I wanted to do. I had enough awareness and confidence to know that I didn't look any different than the girls I saw in the magazines, but I was worried about the nature of the jobs. This girl I had met at the bookstore had told me how one day they were brought to a house outside of Kyoto and just asked to stand or sit around posing and drinking. Their job was just to hang out and create casual scene shots. But I wondered if that could present safety concerns too. I didn't know the language, I had no connections in that industry and I was basically afraid. I ended up not showing up for the appointment though I often wondered where it might have led me. I did enjoy fashion and all it entailed and I continued to buy magazines and pored over the latest fashion shots every month.

With Kumiko, my student who designed for Perry Ellis and Pierre Cardin

Around this same time I received a call from another potential private student. Her name was Kumiko and she lived nearby. We met at Kobeya Kitchen over coffee and we discussed fees and schedules. It turned out she was a designer for a Tokyo company and she designed collections for Perry Ellis and Pierre Cardin. Kumiko came across as being very sweet and friendly. She chose to have the lessons at my apartment on the weekends and on the first scheduled day she arrived right on time. When I heard the doorbell ring I opened the door and invited her in. She seemed excited but also quite nervous.

"Hello Kumiko. Please come in," I said. I smiled and pointed toward the kitchen.

"Nice to meet you today Kim. How are you?" she asked me as she took a seat at the table and removed her jacket.

"I am fine, thank you," I answered.

I found her English verbal skills to be quite good and I wanted to know more about what her goals were with regards to her learning more English.

"Would you like some tea or something to drink? I also have juice," I offered.

"I will have some juice please," she said.

I took a small carton of orange juice from the fridge and poured her a glass. I placed it on the table in front of her and sat down again.

"So Kumiko, where did you learn to speak English so well?"

"Really? You think I speak English well?" she seemed surprised.

"Yes, you do. You speak very well," I said.

"I learned English in school but I practiced my speaking with foreigners that I have met," she explained.

"So do you want to expand your vocabulary then?" I asked her.

"Yes I think that would be good Kim," she answered. I followed her gaze as she looked around at the tiny kitchen. "You're house is so clean!" she exclaimed.

I smiled politely as I brought out a text book to show her. Kumiko seemed more interested in talking to me socially so I closed the book and let her ask me some questions. Our conversation lasted an hour and during that time I had written down a list of new vocabulary words for her to review and practice later. As she got up to leave, she noticed a small wooden sheep sitting on the counter that I had painted.

"Oh, this is so beautiful!" she said.

"Thank you. I painted it myself," I responded. I had been spending some of my spare time buying paint and craft supplies and doing anything creative that I could get my hands on. She seemed shocked.

"You painted this? Oh, I would love to have it," she said.

Without hesitating I offered it to her.

"Oh Kim. You wouldn't mind?"

"Not at all. Please, if you really like it then you can have it. I don't mind. I'm glad you like it!" I handed her the sheep and she seemed very happy. I was touched that someone would actually like something I had made.

Over the next few months, Kumiko became one of my favourite students. We would often talk on the phone and several times she invited me to join her and friends for a drink at a nearby bar called Wink. I never took her up on her offer but she always asked.

Kumiko was a talented designer and she designed collections each season. One week she called to tell me that she would be missing class the following week because she had to travel to Paris for work. I told her how I had always wanted to go to Paris and how I envied her. I told her to have a great time and to not work too hard.

When she returned from Paris she brought me a gift of a beautiful pill box with a picture of the Eiffel Tower on the front. It was a perfect gift. Kumiko was very generous and always bringing me gifts. One day she brought me a beautiful pink and purple scarf with butterflies on it and matching chopsticks. She wrote me poems and shared her friendship openly and willingly. She was very outgoing and she seemed to delight in my presence. She often complimented me on my hair or my appearance. I was beginning to become embarrassed by her attention although secretly I enjoyed it. Perhaps the most precious gift she gave me were several sketches she had drawn of me wearing Perry Ellis designs. I was amazed at how the sketches were such a striking resemblance to me. It felt special to receive a gift that was so personal and unique. She was fuelling my passion and desire for beauty and fashion. Kumiko was a remarkably talented and creative woman and I wished I could be half as artistic as she was.

During this time I had received yet another request to teach English privately. My new student lived in Momoyamadai, one station away. She was an older woman in her 60's and her name was Momoyo. She had been a well-off housewife and she had travelled around the world until she developed cancer. As she related her story to me, I sat in silence, horrified at her ordeal. When she had a brain tumour removed, her husband consequently kicked her out of their home. She was forced to start over on her own and she then set herself up in an apartment following therapy. She explained to me that she had to relearn many things including how to walk and eat by herself. Her English level had dropped significantly and so she wanted to relearn the language.

As I headed to her home one Saturday afternoon, I was struggling on my bike because I was wearing high heels, which I often did, and it was also very windy and rainy outside. Her apartment was some distance from the train station and so I found it easier to bike to her place. But it was mostly uphill and the weather on this day was not forgiving. As the rain pounded down, I held onto my umbrella in my left hand while I tried to steer with my right hand. As I pumped slowly up the hill, my foot slipped on the wet pedal and my shoe fell off into the street. I stopped, lay down the bike, and ran back to retrieve my shoe. By the time I got back to my bike, my books were soaked right through. Determined, I got back on the bike and rode the rest of the way up the hill. The hillside was covered in bamboo, and it was a picturesque little neighbourhood. When I arrived at her home, Momoyo let me in and invited me to sit at her dining room table, along with her son, daughter-in-law and grandson. With this little group I would teach basic vocabulary and grammar over cake and coffee. I soon found that I would have to modify my lesson plans to suit the different levels of the learners in this group. Her son spoke hardly any English and her grandson and daughter-in-law spoke none at all. I tried to engage her young grandson by beginning with the alphabet. Momoyo seemed to really enjoy relearning English and her effort was sincere, although I noticed that she tired quickly.

The following week, her son Masako and his wife were late. We wandered into her bedroom where she wanted to show me a kimono. I stood in awe, as she explained how the entire wall held built-in drawers where she kept several kimonos. She pulled out a beautiful kimono made from red silk with a pattern of cranes on the fabric.

"Kimono is very expensive in Japan. I have many. Before.....before my....sickness, my husband buy me many kimono..." Momoyo said. She smiled faintly as she reached up and pulled open another drawer which revealed even more kimonos tucked neatly inside.

"I can give you kimono as gift," she offered.

I hesitated. I knew the value of a kimono could reach into the tens of thousands of dollars. Her offer, while generous and sincere, left me feeling very uncomfortable. I felt awkward because I would have loved to receive one but I wasn't sure if she truly realized the enormity of her gesture. I also knew that Momoyo would sometimes say things and then forget. I didn't want her to give me a kimono and then later wonder where it was. Besides, I thought, her daughter-in-law will inherit them and she would probably not appreciate a gaijin walking away with one of them.

"Oh....I couldn't take something so valuable. They are too beautiful to give away," I said to her.

Momoyo led me back into the dining room to wait for her son. We had a cup of tea while we sat and she tried remembering her words. I felt pity for her, yet at the same time, she was a survivor. She taught me that no matter what happens in life you never give up. Life is still worth living in spite of hardship and illness.

The next few days brought heavy rain and getting to and from classes was difficult. Somehow the Japanese people would still look immaculately groomed in the middle of a downpour while I would be covered in rain spots with fly away, dishevelled hair. One day, while I was walking to my Nisso Shoji class, one of the heels broke off my shoe. I stood in the middle of the underground walkway, with people flying past, as I held the heel in the palm of my hand. What am I going to do now? People passing by seemed to hardly notice, for a change, I thought wryly. I had no choice but to break off the other heel and wear both shoes as they were. As I began walking with my broken shoes, people suddenly noticed and I drew many curious glances. I had developed a thicker skin by now and I tried hard not to laugh aloud. I knew I must look absolutely ridiculous. Ah, who cares? I grinned to myself. In some ways, being a foreigner allowed me certain privileges. Because I was a gaijin, I would always be seen as an outsider, as someone different and I didn't have to conform to the same strict standards. My Peter Pan shoes were certainly proof of that.

By the end of September, the rain continued with a fury. Bill and I had recently been given a black and white T.V. set by one of my students. Even though we couldn't really understand what was being said, there were some hilarious programs which kept us entertained. I found it incredible that in a society that was so much more reserved than ours, that their T.V. programming would be so openly sexual. Many shows depicted sex in some form or another, whether it was men painting pictures on women's naked bodies, or people having sex in bath houses. Everything centered around sex and there were several versions of dating shows as well. On Saturday nights at 11:00 p.m., we would watch as a male host would invite a young woman to remove her bikini top and then lie down on a mat. Two or three young men would then paint food images on her body, turning her breasts into poached eggs or her torso would become toast. We laughed at the silliness. It was hard to believe what we were watching. Another program that gave us many hours of side-splitting laughter was watching Dukes of Hazzard with Japanese voiceovers. We howled as Paul Michael Glazer ran around screaming "Bawsoo Hawgoo! Bawsoo Hawgoo!"

But on one particular evening, we were bored watching the same shows over and over and so we switched on a news channel and we immediately saw pictures of strong winds and heavy rain. We kept hearing the word "Osaka" repeated over and over.

Bill sat up straight and turned up the volume although we couldn't understand what was being said. He stared intently at the screen.

"What the heck..........what do you think it means?" I glanced over at Bill, who sat unmoving on the futon.

"Something to do with the weather," he answered. He knew as much as I did, which was basically that it looked like bad weather but we couldn't be sure.

We learned the next morning at the school that a typhoon was headed in our direction. It was a Wednesday and all businesses were closed early for the day as employees scurried around piling sand bags in front of windows. We peeked outside and noticed that many of the neighbouring stores had been busy all night piling sandbags up. They were piled all over the city. We were advised to prepare for 3 days of emergency by packing away fresh bottled drinking water and non-perishable food. The main concern for the Japanese authorities was having people stranded in the city. People were being advised to return home and stay put for as long as necessary. As I too headed home early that day I was frightened as I tried to read the expressions on people's faces on the train. I had never been in a typhoon before and I had no idea what to expect. I knew that typhoons could, if strong enough, cause destruction, flooding and possibly death. Would it have enough strength to blow in our windows or send things flying through them?

I made it back to our apartment and shed my wet clothes. Bill came in shortly after I did and when he walked in the door swung shut with a loud bang. He took off his shoes and they were filled with water! I watched in amazement as Bill poured the water out of his shoes and we both jumped as it hit the floor in the entryway. He had to empty the remaining water out in the sink.

"You're soaked too!" Bill laughed as he looked at my drenched hair.

"I know. It was awful out there. Did you hear the news about the typhoon?" I asked.

"Yeah. We'll turn on the news and see what's happening," Bill said. He sat down beside me on the futon as I switched the T.V. on. We could hear the wind howling outside. We looked out the balcony window and saw the telephone wires swinging wildly, and beer cans were flying down the street. There wasn't a person in sight. We switched back and forth from the window to the T.V. trying to keep on top of how serious the situation was getting. It was a sleepless night as the wind shrieked on.

The worst part was not being properly informed. We did have a radio and there was an English station but there was only music playing. Even though we could see pictures on T.V. we couldn't understand which direction or location the typhoon was at any given moment. As we lay there on the floor there was a loud knock at the front door. Bill and I looked at each other, wondering what idiot would be out in the storm at this time of night. When Bill opened the door he started laughing in disbelief.

"Takahashi, what are you doing here?" Bill stood at the door, shaking his head in disbelief.

"Tonight is English lesson," Takahashi smiled as he answered.

"But I told you not to bother coming tonight because of the typhoon," Bill said. He looked at his student incredulously.

"I'm not worried about typhoon. I have seen many," Takahashi answered with a laugh and a wave of his hand.

Bill led him into the kitchen where I prepared hot coffee. The man was drenched but amazingly his lesson books were dry. I served him coffee and cream cakes and slid the papered door shut to the other room. I lay back down on the futon and continued to watch the T.V. with the volume turned down low. I could hear the wind howling madly outside and I worried about Takahashi getting home safely.

It was midnight when the lesson was over and Bill walked Takahashi down the narrow hallway to the front door.

"Drive your bike carefully," Bill cautioned him.

"Don't worry," he replied. He smiled and buttoned up his coat and pulled his hood over his head. As Takahashi opened the door a force of wind came blowing in. It was dark and very windy. This was not a night to be out bike riding I thought to myself.

"Good night Bill and Kim!" he called as he grabbed his umbrella and ran down the steps.

"Good night!" Bill called after him as he pushed the door shut against the wind.

As the evening wore on, we listened intently as the wind continued to howl outside and battered our front door. An hour or so after Takahashi left, we were sitting on the window seat by the kitchen window and we watched in amazement and some fear as the glass literally began to bend with the force of the wind. The window was made with tiny mesh wires criss-crossed throughout the pane and we were hoping it would be enough reinforcement if the window shattered. Realizing that there was nothing we could physically do, and getting tired, we decided to head to bed in the hope that we might get some rest. We managed to sleep until the early morning and when we woke up we both jumped out of bed and looked out the window. The fences, cars and buildings all looked normal. It was eerily quiet.

"The storm has passed. It didn't hit us bad," Bill said as he peered up and down the street.

I wandered into the kitchen and put on some coffee as I sighed with relief.

We later learned that the typhoon had passed just offshore, about 50 miles out from Osaka and then it had weakened in strength. Had the storm been just a few miles closer inland then the damage would have been devastating. I was just happy it was over. After the storm, the weather began to clear and we looked forward to mild, sunny autumn days ahead.

~

About a month later we were invited by two of our fellow teachers, B.J. and his brother Andy, to meet up with them at an underground restaurant called *Gonenbayashi*. It was in Esaka, quite close to our apartment. It was perhaps a ten minute bike ride down a few side streets. Esaka station itself was almost like a miniature Shinsaibashi station. It had several flashing neon signs, pachinko parlours, high-rise restaurants and a bit of shopping at the nearby Tokyu Hands department store.

Gonenbayashi was located down a flight of several black marble stairs. Inside, the decor was typically Japanese in design and there were tatami rooms with cushions, separated by rice paper doors. On the other side of the restaurant the cooking was done out in the open within a rectangular space. Patrons could sit on stools if they chose, around the kitchen, and watch their food being prepared. The first day of every month was half price on everything, food and alcohol. You had to make reservations as the place became hugely popular for Japanese people and foreigners alike.

It was November 1st and on this evening there must have been about 20 of us teachers and some administrators and salesmen from

Interac. We sat on our cushions around wide pine tables as the dishes were brought out. The food was incredibly delicious. We ordered fried rice, which had a spicy flavour, bacon wrapped in miniature shiitake mushrooms, deep fried chicken and marinated tomatoes. Our favourite part was the *chu-hai* served with the meal. Chu-Hai is a potent mixture of sake and mango juice. It tastes like pop but the sake numbs your head within a few minutes.

We all stood up as the chu-hai drinks were passed around. B.J., the comedian, started singing parody songs from Australia. Then, divided into two groups, we did the 'boat race'. Every team member began drinking their chu-hai as fast as possible, one person at a time. When the last person on the team finished gulping their drink, we all cheered "chu-hai!". After two rounds we were all so drunk it became hilarious just watching to see who could remain standing. We joined in with Andy and B.J., singing Australian songs that we quickly learned, and dancing around the table. People throughout the restaurant joined in and we separated into teams based on our home countries. After several more drinking rounds, Canada was declared the winner, beating out even the Australians, who always seemed to be the rival when pitted against the Canadians with drinking.

By the time Bill and I left the restaurant, we were plastered. We managed, somehow, to find our bikes and head toward home. I was on a race to beat him as I zoomed off and left him behind at a red light.

"Ha ha!" I yelled as I continued speeding down the road.

At that moment a Toyota sedan pulled alongside of me. A man, evidently drunk, began shouting obscenities at me and whistling. If I had been sober I probably would have turned around and rode back to Bill but in my current state I wasn't thinking with a clear head. So, full of alcohol induced bravado, I lowered my head to his passenger window and swore at him in Japanese. I was sure that he understood me and apparently he did, because when I turned the corner onto the road that would take me straight to our apartment, he sped ahead and turned the car sideways so that it blocked the road.

As I got closer, I had two choices I thought to myself. Either I keep on going and run right into him, which would be dangerous, or I could stop, but that could be worse because I couldn't be sure of what his intentions were. I decided to go for it and so I kept on pedalling directly toward him. I figured he would be hurt more than I would and there was no way I was going to stop for this insane man. He was standing in front of the car with his pants open, talking incoherently as he stared straight at me. I was shocked by his behaviour but I was also feeling angry. I was sick and tired of being viewed as a sex object, something to push around, something seen as less worthy. I had had enough and I was going to lash out and retaliate. I pedalled faster and as I came within three or four feet of him he then quickly ducked to the side of the road. I instantly made a sharp right hand turn and I barely made it between the front end of his car and the chain link fence.

My heart was pounding but I didn't stop pedalling. I rode as fast as I could and when I saw our apartment building, I was thinking that I had to somehow get inside without this crazy man seeing where I lived. I managed to turn into the driveway and I hid behind the other bikes until I saw the reflection of his headlights approaching. I held my breath as I watched his car drive off down the road. I chained up my bike and, shakily, I ran up the stairs to our apartment. I was still out of breath, and I peeked over the railing just to make sure he was gone. As I entered the apartment, I was wondering frantically where Bill was. He shouldn't have been that far behind me. Just then the front door opened and Bill came in. I jumped up as he came into the kitchen and I told him what had happened.

"Are you okay?" Bill was drunk but his concern was written all over his face.

I nodded.

"I thought I noticed a car slow down outside of our apartment," Bill said. He went over to the window and looked out.

"You need to be careful Kim. Keep your eyes open in case he comes around again," Bill warned. I could tell that Bill wasn't happy about this situation and neither was I. I could only hope that this creep didn't know where I lived. Both of us realized the potential danger and we recalled how the two young women from the States, Lisa and Barbara, woke in the middle of the night to find a strange man in their apartment. On another occasion their underwear was stolen off of their clothesline on their balcony. That incident had left them shaken and fearing for their safety as well.

Afterwards, I would only chase Bill on the bike in the day time. Esaka was not the safest area to be alone in at night because of the proximity to the yakusa, the Japanese mafia, many of whom lived in Esaka.

Another element of gangs in Japan are the *bosozoku*, young wan-nabes, working their way up the ladder for a life of crime. They were basically a juvenile version of the yakusa and they drove around the city on their motor bikes. Sometimes they would park in front of our apartment building in the dead of night and rev up their engines with an "ER, ER, ERRRRRRRR" sound coming from the high pitch of the engines. Most people were afraid to confront the bosozoku and we had even seen the police being chased by them on occasion.

It was at the end of November that I had become ill with the flu and my head was pounding relentlessly one day. It was 3:00 in the after-noon when, trying to sleep, I heard a biker revving up his engine right outside my window. It went on steadily for quite some time until finally, my head feeling like it would split open, I opened the sliding door and stepped out onto the balcony. I hurled 3 plastic bags full of garbage down below.

"How do you expect anyone to sleep!" I yelled down at them. "I can't even be sick in peace!"

As I looked down below me, I saw one of the bags land with a THUD right beside one of the bikers. As he turned to look my way, another of the bags hit him square on the back of his head. With that, I ducked down and backed into the room, thinking that I shouldn't have done what I just did. But as soon as I heard his bike screech away I relaxed and crawled back onto my futon. I shut my eyes and fell into a peace-ful sleep.

CHAPTER 8

The Monkeys of Shodo-Shima

A nother Christmas season was on its way. We decided this year that we wanted to celebrate and be with other people. The year before had been so lonely and lacked Christmas spirit as we had to work. Our company now recognized Christmas as an important holiday for us foreign teachers and we were given two weeks off.

Knowing we had several days off, we decided to make full use of our free time and so we made several plans. We invited 3 other teachers to join us for Christmas holiday on Shodo-Shima, otherwise known as Monkey Island, where we had heard about a Japanese family who lived there and who had imported logs from Canada and built a perfect log home. Apparently, they frequently rented out the log home as a sort of novel tourist attraction for people wanting to stay in a real Canadian log cabin. We thought this was a great idea and a very appropriate way to spend the holiday.

The teachers that were joining us were Ellen, Brian and his wife Lisa, all of whom were from the United States. Brian and Lisa were from the Boston area and Ellen was from New Jersey. We met up at Umeda station early one morning and we took a train from there to the port of Osaka. From there we walked to the ferry terminal where we had a four hour boat ride to Shodo-Shima.

The weather was grey and damp but despite the chill in the air, we were all excited about getting away for Christmas. I had suggested to each of them that we all bring a wrapped gift which we could exchange on Christmas Eve. The idea I had was that we could play a card game that my family often did on Christmas Eve and we could 'steal' gifts from each other as our cards were called out by the dealer. I thought it might be a fun addition to our Christmas celebration.

As we settled down on the floor at the front of the ferry, I looked over at Ellen. She had pulled out her gift, wrapped in red tissue paper.

"Gee, I wonder if anyone will guess what this is!" she chuckled as she held up the bag. Anyone could see it was a mug. She had a really great sense of humour. She was from New Hampshire, where she had worked as a nurse. Ellen was in her 30's, and she had short brown hair and a smiling face. You could tell from the upturned crinkle by her eyes that she spent a lot of time smiling. Her manner was warm and friendly.

"Well now, I haven't got a clue what's in your bag!" I laughed as I stared at the small package sitting on her lap.

"Hey Lisa, did you remember to bring a gift?" I looked in her direction. She was leaning back against the wall, trying to get comfortable.

"I sure did. It was a great idea, by the way," she said.

Bill and Brian started chatting and we alternately slept, played cards and talked throughout the trip to pass the time. I noticed how none of the Japanese passengers sat in the same room that we were in. I went for a walk and was looking for a bathroom, peering into other rooms along the way. Each room was packed full of people while our room was nearly empty. That's strange, I thought.

Upon reaching Shodo-Shima, we were picked up at the terminal by Nobuyuki, the owner of the log cabin. His young daughter was with him. As we drove to the cabin, I stared out the window at the passing countryside. It was so green here, so unlike Osaka. As we got closer, we could see the cabin perched on the hill, like a temple. It was huge, newly built, and so Canadian looking.

As we were invited inside, we entered with a collective gasp. It was massive inside, with a high, open-beamed ceiling. The floors were brightly polished and there was an immense, long wooden pine table in the center of the room. Nobuyuki's wife had put out cute little Christmas decorations for us. I was very touched by her gesture. Upstairs, there was a large loft with a tatami floor. We were shown a narrow cupboard on the side of the loft where we could find our futons.

"Welcome," Nobuyuki said as he spread his arms and gestured around the cabin. "You can use the toilet in the main house," he added. He motioned for us to follow him into the living room of the cabin.

"We have karaoke here. Please use if you like. Make yourself comfortable. Please be clean," he said politely. He seemed to want us to be relaxed and he was very hospitable. His daughter stood quietly beside him, watching us with curiosity.

As we all stood there, Ellen opened her jacket and pulled out a ferret. Unbeknownst to me, she had promised a friend to look after it while this woman went back home for a couple of weeks. When Ellen had first brought the ferret out of her bag on the ferry ride over we were stunned. Now we wondered what Nobuyuki would think. I looked over at him and saw his eyes express shock.

"He's harmless.....and potty trained," Ellen said. She looked over at Nobuyuki as the rest of us just stood in complete silence.

Nobuyuki's daughter looked on with horror at the little animal wriggling in Ellen's arms. She shrank back and stood behind her father as she giggled nervously.

"What...what is this animal?" Nobuyuki asked as he pointed at the ferret.

"This is a ferret. He 's very friendly. Would you like to pet him?" Ellen asked as she extended the animal toward him.

Nobuyuki hesitated for a moment. Many Japanese people are very fond of animals and we had met several people who illegally kept small cats and dogs in their apartments. After a moment, Nobuyuki stepped forward, ever so slowly, and gently pet the animal on its head. His daughter, seeing the animal was friendly, began giggling uncontrollably. She too, stepped closer and raised her hand and began petting the ferret.

Once we realized that everything was okay, we began to unpack our food and clothing. Nobuyuki invited us to pick Japanese oranges in his orchard if we hadn't any other plans. We were open to any new experience and so we eagerly piled into his truck and drove down to his orchard. There were orange trees growing right up the side of the mountain. Nobuyuki demonstrated for us how to pick the oranges and then told us to go ahead and have fun. I walked over to a nearby tree and gently pulled the orange off as I held the stem. I ran over to another tree and did the same thing again. I stood grinning in my sweat pants, holding two oranges I had just picked as Bill took a picture. What a unique experience we all thought. We enjoyed ourselves despite the biting coldness in the air. It had started to rain and the dampness seemed to penetrate into our clothes and seep into our bones. We were all shivering. Nobuyuki, an excellent host, could see that we were becoming tired and so he drove us back to the cabin where he built us a delightful fire. When he finished, he left us to warm up, promising to visit with us later on.

Celebrating Christmas on Shodo-Shima, December 1990

Harvesting Japanese oranges on Shodo-Shima

The next two days were wonderful. We spent the first evening drinking and singing karaoke. Nobuyuki, as promised, did return with his daughter and they sat with us for the entire evening. He brought over a bottle of *sho-chu*, a sake drink with a poisonous snake pickled at the bottom of the bottle. I declined his repeated offers to take a drink from it as the bottle got passed around the table. Our singing was atrocious, but we were carefree and having fun, relaxing and drinking with abandon. The next day was Christmas.

We woke up early, yawning, and we all lay there, curled up in our warm futons.

"Merry Christmas!" Bill said loudly. We all wished each other a merry Christmas in turn, and it felt like we were the Walton's family. We forced ourselves to get up and Lisa began making breakfast in the kitchen. We sat down together for a meal of bacon, eggs and toast.

Surrounded by monkeys on Shodo-Shima

Later in the morning, Nobuyuki drove us further up to 'monkey mountain' to see the incredible view of the ocean. We continued climbing up the mountain, all of us squeezed into his van when suddenly there was a THUD! on the roof of the vehicle. There followed a high-pitched screeching noise and we all froze in terror. I was sitting in the front passenger seat and I instinctively looked over at Nobuyuki but he appeared intent and focused on driving straight ahead, although he did slow down. As I looked up at the top of the windshield I instantly let out a scream "AAAAAAHHHHHH! My God, what *is* that?" I pointed and shrunk back in my seat in fear. Nobody answered as we all stared out the windows in shock. I was shaking, certain that the creature that was staring directly into my face would smash the windshield and attack us all. It curled its humanlike fingers as though it was trying to pick off the glass windshield.

"Just stay calm," Nobuyuki said. He stopped driving as many more monkeys scrambled down the mountainside and onto the vehicle and on every side of us on the road.

"There are many monkeys here. They can be dangerous but they won't harm us if we sit quietly," he added. Nobuyuki acted calm but he seemed frightened to me. We all sat in silence as the engine idled. The monkeys were surrounding the vehicle, some clinging onto the sides and more were climbing onto the roof and the front hood. They were aggressive and curious. Nobuyuki slowly started moving the vehicle again as monkeys continued to climb down the mountain toward us.

When we reached the top of the mountain I was afraid to get out of the van. Eventually we all piled out , checking over our shoulders, expecting an ambush any moment.

"Walk with your hands up in the air. They will then see that you have nothing. They like to steal things from people. Hide anything you have in your pocket. Walk slowly and do not act afraid," Nobuyuki instructed us as he led us away from the van.

Was he kidding us? Why were we putting ourselves at risk just for a view? I stuck as close to Bill as I possibly could, trying to use him as a shield. Nobuyuki was trying to be helpful but my fear only intensified the further away we were from the van.

We walked along a trail toward the lookout point. We came to a clearing where there were several monkeys huddling together in a tight circle. It looked like they were having a meeting over how to handle us humans who were invading their territory. I watched, fascinated, as a mother sat with her baby, plucking parasites out of its hair and then grooming her baby's hair with patience. Every couple of minutes or so, a male monkey would approach us from behind, screeching it presence but, as we were advised to do, we simply help up our hands and the monkeys would become bored and scamper away.

We continued walking along the trail and finally we reached the lookout point where we walked out to a gazebo perched on the edge of the cliff. The sky overhead was oddly dark despite the early hour of the day. We gazed out at the ocean, noticing the oyster farms far below in the water. We could make out the giant nets used for harvesting the oysters. These pearls would be exported all over the world.

A strong gust of wind came up and I bundled up my jacket and tried to pull it up high to protect my ears from the biting coldness. After several minutes we decided to return to the van. We all piled in once again but on the way down we asked Nobuyuki if he would let us off as we wanted to go exploring on our own.

"Let you off here?" he asked.

We all nodded as though we wouldn't have it any other way.

"Well okay. It is nice day for a walk. It is not far to go back to my cabin. Have a good walk," he said. We watched as he drove off, wondering where we should walk to.

We hiked down the mountain and walked along the highway until we came to a small fishing village. The houses were clustered together, with their blue tiled roofs sloping upwards and the balconies were all decorated with potted plants. It was an idyllic setting, a very quaint village.

After awhile the cold was getting to us and we were hungry. It had been about 3 hours since Nobuyuki dropped us off and we wondered how far we had to go until we would reach the cabin.

Ellen looked especially tired. "Nobuyuki said it wasn't a far walk," she said.

I nodded as I looked down at my feet. "My feet are going to be frozen by the time we make it back." My hands and feet were incredibly cold and the wind was chilling my face. All of us spoke little, trying to keep warm as best we could. We walked for about another hour before finally the cabin came into view.

"Hooray!" Lisa shouted and we all quickened our pace, anxious to get inside and get warmed up.

Bill opened the door and a rush of warm air came blowing out. The ferret crawled out from behind a ceiling beam, disturbed by the sudden noise. We trundled in and removed our heavy coats and shoes. It was time to start preparing dinner. Our Christmas dinner would be spaghetti, made with Ellen's seafood sauce. We would have chocolate cake for dessert. While dinner was cooking we lounged around the table, munching on Japanese oranges and singing karaoke.

We ate hungrily, savouring the small amount of sauce that was sparingly divided between the five of us. Although our food and music was not traditional for the Christmas holiday, it was a real satisfying and festive atmosphere. It really felt like Christmas after all, and we cheerfully drank our beer as we danced around the table.

We exchanged our presents later that evening. Though the gifts were not extravagant, they brought us pleasure and it felt good to be involved in a Christmas tradition so far away from home. I think, for the first time in my life, I appreciated a deeper meaning of giving. When things aren't so readily available you can enjoy the simplicity much more easily. We looked at our array of coffee mugs and calendars as though they were the best presents on earth. There was one gift left unopened. When Nobuyuki and his daughter joined us later on that evening, we gave Nobuyuki's daughter the unopened, wrapped box. Her eyes opened wide in astonishment and she lit up with excitement as she held the box in her hand. We encouraged her to open it and we explained that traditionally we gave presents to others at Christmas time. Her eyes sparkled with delight as she unopened the box. She took her time and opened it very carefully. She drew in her breath when she saw the mug. She seemed to view the mug as a valuable jewel but I think really for her it was the novelty and excitement of celebrating Christmas for the first time.

It had been a long and tiring day. I had briefly called my parents from the antique phone in the entryway of the cabin. The combination of companionship, sharing gifts and hearing my family's voices left me feeling lighthearted and grateful for a chance to have Christmas again.

We left Shodo-Shima the next afternoon and we did our best to leave the cabin as spotless as when we arrived. The ferry ride was tedious and the weather in Osaka was dark and gloomy. Bill and I had thoroughly enjoyed Shodo-Shima and now we were looking forward to celebrating New Year's at Machiko's home, a lady who was one of my private students.

Celebrating New Year's with Sawako and her family

New Year's is an important holiday in Japan. Traditionally, the shops would close for one week and the women would prepare food in advance by spending endless days cooking and storing food for the holiday. It was a time for family and for resting from a long year of working.

Today many people in Japan travel to foreign countries for their New Year's holiday. They get so little time off work so it is an ideal time to travel. Another factor is their families are often so widely spread out in different cities that they don't always get the opportunity to get together. Machiko and her daughter Sawako invited us to their apartment for a traditional Japanese New Year's meal. When we arrived at their apartment we were a few minutes early. Machiko was dressed elaborately, with glamorous make up. Her husband and daughter were similarly well dressed. I felt embarrassed at our casual dress in sweaters and jeans. Machiko invited us in and gestured for us to sit on the tatami floor of her dining room. There were five miniature black lacquered tables set out in front of us. Arranged meticulously on the tables were shrimp, eggs, roe and pickled ginger root. Each item held a symbolic meaning.

Bill threw me a little smile as we politely gazed at our 'meal'. I knew Bill would be starving after this. We sipped our red wine as we toasted each other "Kanpai!" I didn't know where to start eating as I wasn't sure about the etiquette with regards to which item to eat first. Ginger root? Fish eggs? I settled on the shrimp and as I devoured the one piece off my tray, Machiko leaned over to me.

"Shrimp mean long life. See the back? It look like old woman!" she laughed heartily at her own joke.

"You can eat eggs. Fish eggs mean..........many children!" Sawako grinned with mischief. Her short cropped hair framed her face and she gave off an air of a comedienne. She had an outgoing and happy personality. Both mother and daughter were constantly telling jokes. Although sometimes their jokes were lost on me, their body language was infectious. I began laughing too as I speared the fish eggs with my chopstick wondering how I was going to eat it without grimacing.

During our meal, Bill was struggling to keep his legs crossed for such a long period of time and at one point he tried shifting his legs to ease the cramps he was feeling. Because he had such long legs, when he moved his knee it hit the edge of his little table and his food and drink spilled all over the tatami mat. It was an embarrassing moment as Machiko rushed to clean the mess up. Machiko's husband just grinned as he pointed at Bill's legs and made a gesture with his hands that meant 'big legs, big feet'. Afterwards we laughed about this and our hosts were very good sports about it.

After dinner, we listened to classical Japanese music and drank beer. Sawako showed me her room with its bunk bed, a small closet and Jon Bon Jovi posters all over the wall. She was a funny girl and she was so unlike the slim and nervous schoolgirls I mostly encountered. She was athletic, very witty and she seemed energized whenever she tried to speak English with a foreigner. She was a warm and wonderful girl.

Sometime after midnight we wished each other a Happy New Year as we embraced and kissed each other. It had been a fun, entertaining night.

"Bye Keemoo. See you.....next Saturday!" Machiko's cheeks glowed red from the wine and she struggled to speak her English words correctly.

"Bye Beel! Thank you for coming tonight!" Machiko said.

Bill bowed to Machiko, her husband and to Sawako, causing her to laugh uncontrollably.

We left their apartment, climbed on our bikes and pedalled home in the dark. Wow, it was 1991! I was now twenty-four years old and had celebrated another New Year's Eve birthday in Japan. I reflected that so much had happened in our first year and I wondered - what would the second year bring?

CHAPTER 9

Thailand and the Gulf War

With Christmas and New Year's winding down, we had a trip to Thailand to look forward to. I was beginning to feel an inner happiness that was very comforting not only for my body but for my mind. After having several days off from work and the constant grind of commuting back and forth from companies all over Osaka, I was relaxed and full of new energy. We had money now to spend compared to the previous year and if we wanted to visit a temple or visit a different city we could now afford the excursion and an enjoyable lunch out.

Bill and I were scheduled to leave for Bangkok on January 16th and so I thought that I should buy a bathing suit and some new holiday clothes. Early one afternoon I took the Midosuji subway to Umeda which was one of my favourite shopping districts. There was a large mall across from the station which was full of good quality and reasonably priced goods. There were mostly clothing and accessory shops for women which I often went to. On paydays I would typically cash my cheque for ¥220,000.00 and head to the mall. I was beginning to learn my way around pretty good by now and I had sourced out boutique stores which carried clothing and shoes in my size. I would buy suits, lingerie, shoes, umbrellas, make up, basically anything that I felt that I needed. It wasn't unusual for me to spend two or three hundred dollars on a blouse. But I would always keep a look out for any bargains that I could find and on one occasion I found a pair of shoes for CDN$40.00. I always felt like I had hit the jackpot when I could find nice clothing for under CDN$100.00. Clothing was much more expensive in Japan than it was in Canada but the quality was ten times better. Gradually my closet began to fill up with my new purchases. Just as Bill found his pleasure in playing Pachinko, my joy was in practicing the art of being a loyal customer.

Umeda was one of the busiest stations in all of Osaka and there were stairways and walkways leading in every direction. Underground coffee houses were scattered around every corner, wedged in between department stores, banks and kiosks of every kind. The noises of the subway trains and thousands of people were always present. People would elbow each other as they tried to find space to walk. Above ground there was the same frenzy as thousands of people came out to shop for the afternoon. Everywhere you looked you could see concrete buildings and neon signs. After heading out of the subway I crisscrossed the street thinking about which store I would look in first. As I continued my search for a bathing suit for Thailand I wandered past a lingerie boutique that looked like it had nice things inside. Would I possibly find a bathing suit in there I wondered? I could see displays of beautiful lingerie so I went in and began looking around. I gazed at the hardwood floors and the tables edged in brass upon which were perfectly folded nightgowns and negligees. Against the wall there were mahogany bureaus which were covered with neatly folded panties and bras. I always admired the decor in many of the stores and they were clean and aesthetically pleasing. As I approached the bras a plump Japanese woman immediately came up to me and asked what size I wore. I was somewhat surprised by her question because when I usually went into a store the employees would hover behind their counters with their hands over their mouths as they giggled while I browsed. When this happened I would try my best to ignore their behaviour and try to find what I needed. This woman, however, had a very different approach. I already knew that Japanese sizes were different from North American sizes so I was trying to figure out what my bra size would be and I wasn't sure. I tried to ignore her request.

"Size-wa deska?" she asked, looking impatient.

"Sumimasen.....ano....size-wa.....American size," I responded. I tried my best to communicate but I wasn't sure it was successful. I was also feeling frustrated and tired and I didn't feel like I had the energy to explain with my limited Japanese skills.

She pushed me into a tiny cubicle and motioned for me to remove my blouse. She then took the tape measure from around her neck and wrapped it tightly around my chest. Finally, she reached out for my left breast and squeezed it!

"Uhhh.....chotto motte kudasai!" I stepped backward as I raised my arm protectively in front of me. As I turned, my face flushed bright red, I noticed several young men who had come into the store and they were standing there staring at my chest. I quickly drew back the curtain and threw on my blouse. I stalked out of the store, too embarrassed to even look back.

Eventually, I made it to one of my favourite clothing boutiques where I found a pair of shorts that fit and some casual tight-fitting shirts that were currently in style. I also managed to find a bathing suit that would suffice even though it wasn't the style I was hoping for. As I walked back through the mall I saw a shoe store that I sometimes patronized. There were several comfortable, stylish boots in suede that I knew would be perfect for my weekend tourist trips to Kyoto. I always had to cross my fingers that they had my size and when I saw a pair in the right size, my heart skipped as I happily paid for them and walked out feeling successful. With my new clothes and shoes in hand I walked through Umeda station to catch the Midosuji train back home.

On the train I sat with a triumphant smile on my face. I loved shopping days! Looking down at my new purchases in their fancy packaging I felt satisfied. I remembered the floral umbrella and matching raincoat that I had bought the month before and I was proud of them too. It had taken me some time to feel that I was as well dressed as the Japanese women and now my confidence was high.

~

Bill and I left Osaka International Airport on a dark and rainy afternoon on January 16th. Although it was a long flight to Thailand we were happy to be heading to the sun and enjoying our free time together. We arrived in Bangkok in the evening and we planned to spend the night there before flying to Phuket Island the following day.

We claimed our baggage and headed out of the terminal into the warm night air. Climbing into a taxi we sped off into the snarl of traffic as we each stared out the window, trying to see what we could. Bangkok was a large city with old rusty buses barrelling down the potholed streets as they spewed out diesel fumes. People were everywhere on the streets, walking, riding in cars or on mopeds, darting in and out of traffic in an almost suicidal manner. We saw people selling fried fruit from little carts on the sidewalks and I wished that we had more time to stay so we could explore the city. We also wanted to go on the river where tourists could take a scenic ride in boats. We could see glimpses of the river on nearly every street we drove down and here and there we saw large golden statues and monuments that were set on the banks of the river. We finally got to our hotel which was a rundown place and I was suddenly grateful that we would not be there for more than one night. The room was dingy and outdated but we were so tired we eagerly climbed into bed, anticipating the beauty of Phuket Island.

Early the next morning we ate a quick continental breakfast and took a taxi back to the airport. We boarded a small plane and as we flew to Phuket Island we could see the beauty of the aquamarine water below and the lush green vegetation dotted with palm trees. It looked like paradise.

Arriving on Phuket Island, we encountered a very small airport and yet even in such a seemingly tranquil environment there were several armed soldiers standing about with their sub-machine guns strapped to their shoulders. I glanced at Bill who seemed as shocked as I was. I had never before seen armed soldiers in a public environment. We learned that the air assault of the Gulf War had just broken out but we still didn't understand yet why the war would have an effect here. As we absorbed this information and tried to discern if we may be in any potential danger, we were approached by a beautiful young Thai woman who held out a binder to us. It was full of coloured photos of hotels and different huts that catered to tourists. Our hotel in Bangkok had been arranged in advance but we had not booked a place to stay on Phuket Island. We both were amazed at such a brilliant idea that really simplified the ordeal of finding a place to stay. The woman was exceedingly friendly and polite as she gave us suggestions. After looking through the binder, we chose to stay in some bungalows located on Kata Beach near Club Med. The woman immediately called the hotel's reservation number and booked our room for us.

As we drove to Kata Beach we could see endless groves of rubber trees which stretched out nearly to the edge of the road. The air was warm and sweet smelling without any noticeable humidity. The road suddenly began winding down toward the water below us.

Kata Beach appeared to be a touristy but quaint place with jeeps and mopeds piled high with foreign tourists as they roared past, likely on their way to some out of the way beach. We saw shops everywhere and it was a hopping vibrant little town. The hotels and huts were built around several small coves around the shoreline. Our bungalow was on top of a small hill, surrounded with flowers and vegetation. After checking in we were anxious to get out and explore so we decided to wander down to the beach to go snorkelling. The beach was absolutely stunning. The water was warm and crystal clear and very clean. As we floated on the water, our masks and snorkels on, we saw a huge variety of coloured fish swimming beneath the surface.

After drying out in the sun we returned to our bungalow and changed into some clean clothes. We wanted to wander the streets and see what there was to see. There were several rustic shops scattered about and as we strolled through some of them we began to notice that many of the shop's owners had their T.V.'s tuned in to a local news station.

"That news can't be related to the Gulf War Bill, those pictures look local," I said as I pointed to a T.V. set back on a counter. I couldn't help but notice, however, that they kept showing pictures of Middle Eastern people and the word 'Thailand' repeatedly. I wondered what that was all about. The shop owner smiled at us as he pointed to the T.V.

"You no worry. This war far away. Thailand very safe," he reassured us.

We left the shop with the owner crying out "Thailand nice place!"

We both turned back around and smiled at him.

After seeing so many tourists riding motorbikes we decided we would give it a try and go for a spin. We quickly found a rental shop and after signing our lives away I hopped on the back behind Bill. I laughed as he pushed in the throttle but would stall the bike. I sat there, hanging on to him until he finally got it going and we took off down the hill. The shops and beaches soon disappeared and we were on a winding narrow road densely edged with trees. I knew we weren't too far from the resorts but I had an uneasy feeling. We passed two shacks and as we peered in we could see several men sitting on the ground and on the little porch, their rusty trucks parked nearby.

"Bill, I think we should turn around," I said. I looked behind me anxiously.

"What for?" He pushed the throttle down further as the bike picked up speed.

"We don't know who those guys are. Maybe this is a private road," I said. They sure hadn't looked friendly when we had passed them. Perhaps they weren't friendly. But who could blame them? They may have felt resentful toward the huge numbers of tourists with their money or maybe they were involved with the drug trade. I didn't have a clear guess but I had that inner feeling in my gut that those guys were not good. What bothered me was that I couldn't see any other tracks in the dirt and there was only one road here. There were no side roads to turn off in case we needed to. There was one way in and one way out. I squeezed Bill's waist nervously.

"Bill, please. Just turn around. Let's ride along one of the main roads," I suggested.

"What are you afraid of? I want to explore and see what there is to see," he answered. He seemed impatient with my fears and he continued further down the road but he finally slowed down the bike and turned it around. As we neared the shacks again I could see a couple of the men leaning against their trucks as they looked in our direction. Had they been planning to follow us down the road? I had no idea but I was following my instincts and glad that I did. Soon the road widened and was paved again and I breathed a sigh of relief. We rode through the streets to the other end of town before returning the bike.

After our bike ride through the jungle, we thought it might be a good idea to head back to the beach and relax for awhile before dinner. As we lay on the beach we saw a young Thai man pull up on the shore on a jet ski. I thought it would be fun to be able to take a spin and wondered idly if there would be a place where I could rent one nearby. A short while later I went back out to swim and this same young man pulled up beside me on his jet ski.

"You want to go for ride?" he was quite young looking, maybe 18 or 19 I guessed.

"How much?" I looked up at him as I asked.

"I take you for ride for free. You can see beautiful water," he said. He smiled and seemed friendly. I wondered why he was offering to give me a ride and yet not charge money. I didn't realize at my young age how naive I could be sometimes. I figured he was being nice and so waving at Bill, who sat looking on, I agreed and climbed on the back as he stretched out his hand.

"Just a quick ride, okay?" I didn't want to go too far.

"No problem lady. We stay right here in the bay," he said as he waved his arm around to indicate the small bay we were now in.

As we sped off I realized that I didn't even know his name. I glanced back over my shoulder at Bill and I thought that as long as he was around I would be fine. I had no real reason to be worried until he started for the peninsula that jutted out at the end of the bay. I quickly realized that he was planning on going around the point and therefore out of sight. I suddenly felt very uneasy and I noticed that he had tensed his body up and was driving much faster.

I yelled into his ear "I think we've gone far enough! I want to go back now!"

He didn't turn around but he pointed ahead. "Just a moment, you will see very beautiful bay and then I promise we will turn around," he said.

I didn't like this situation at all. As we turned around the point I could see a large rusty old barge that was tilted in the water and had evidently been there for some time. I began to feel panicky, something wasn't right about this.

"Can we please go back now?" I hoped he didn't hear the anxiety in my voice.

He continued driving toward the barge and as I glanced up at it I saw two dark male heads peer out from one of the rusted portholes. We were slowly circling the barge and I knew I was in a dangerous situation. I had to stay focused but my heart was racing.

"Okay, let's go back *now,*" I said. I spoke as firmly and calmly as I was capable of.

"You can meet my friends. We can just go on boat and say hi for few minutes," he said.

I had to think quickly. I could jump off the jet-ski but they would only swim after me. Three men against one woman, I had no chance. This bay was completely deserted, there was no one on the shore and no visible buildings. All I could think of was that they were planning on assaulting me or kidnapping me for smuggling. I knew that even though I was twenty-four years old I looked more like I could be seventeen or eighteen. I had to use my head and use it fast. I was scared.

"No! We must go back *now* or my husband will be *very* worried. He will become angry and he will call the police if I don't get back *right away*," I insisted. I only hoped that I sounded convincing. He slowed the jet ski down alongside the barge and I told him again how angry my husband would be and that he would come looking for me very soon. Finally, perhaps believing my story, he seemed to decide that I wasn't worth the risk and so he waved to his friends and he turned the jet ski around. I almost started to cry with relief. I found it strange that this guy would acknowledge that he had friends on the barge but still they remained hidden and out of sight.

As we drove back into the bay where we had come from I could see Bill standing on the edge of the water looking for me. The guy stopped the jet ski several feet from shore and I jumped off and swam to shore without looking back once. The second I came ashore I ran up to Bill, shaking with relief. He was worried about me.

"What's wrong? Where did you go?" he asked.

As I explained to him what had happened, he hugged me tightly and I calmed down, realizing how stupid I had been in trusting a total stranger. If I had been nervous about aspects of southern Asia before, I was now far less trusting and I felt on edge.

In the evening we had a nice dinner of coconut rice and lobster with sweet chili sauce. I found the food to be delicious and very spicy. After dinner, we retreated to our bungalow for the night.

The following day was enjoyable and relaxing. Rising early, we had a light breakfast of fresh fruit and juice before strolling through the little town. We were looking for a local clinic as we had both been afflicted with a mild stomach ailment common to travellers in this area. Finding the clinic was easy as the town was quite small. We waited maybe 10 minutes before seeing the doctor, who prescribed stomach pills for both of us. We then bought a few souvenirs and some music tapes from some of the local vendors. Following a lunch of coconut flavoured rice and noodles, we spent a beautiful afternoon on the beach where I went para-sailing. Seeing the unique craggy outlines of the rocks from up above was spectacular. If I could ever have imagined a perfect vacation day then this would be it. Bill and I played a game of football with a coconut as other beachgoers dozed topless in the sun. We were getting gorgeous tans and we were happy and full of life. We decided that we would take a ferry boat to Phi-Phi Don Island the next morning. We were told that there were no roads on the island, minimal electrical services and perhaps 200 to 300 locals living on the island.

The next morning, we took the small ferry over to the island and as we pulled into the little bay it was like entering a tropical wonderland. The boat docked at a small pier and as we walked toward shore we gazed at the stunning view of this tiny village set among tall palm trees. The beach area was spotless with the impossibly clear water lining the edge of the sand. It was calm, picturesque, and undeveloped. This same beach would be wiped out and the small structures that we gazed upon now would be gone many years later after the horrific tsunami that came crashing into the island in December 2004.

Bill relaxing at Charlie's Beach in Thailand

The fish market on Phi Phi Don Island, Thailand

Phi-Phi Don Island had literally one unpaved road along which tourists could find small family- run restaurants serving local seafood. The seafood was caught fresh every morning and hung on large hooks in front of the shops or arrayed neatly on wooden tables. My mouth watered as we walked passed large red lobsters, crabs, giant prawns, and fish of every size and shape. There were also souvenir shops selling bamboo mats, silk scarves and T-shirts. We saw a poster advertising boat tours to the swallow caves where men climb steep bamboo ladders in the caves and collect bird's nests which are then exported to China and used in special dishes. Now this seemed like a fun way to spend an afternoon. We signed up for an excursion for the following day. Leaving the main road, we wandered along a sandy path and after crossing through some bush we came upon a group of little huts with dirt floors sitting on the top of a hill above a creek. We took a quick look and kept walking. About five minutes further down the path we came out into a beautiful clearing of palm trees with the turquoise water in the distance. There were several large A-framed huts scattered along the beach. A sign stood nearby that read "Charlie's Beach". We approached the reservation counter which was housed in a little hut under a straw roof. We asked about accommodations.

"We have large huts with living area, bathroom and bedroom. They are good price," the man told us.

"Do they have dirt floors?" Bill asked.

"No. The floors are concrete, very clean. They are US$20.00 per night," he answered.

Bill and I looked at each other. Well that was an obvious choice.

"We'll take one," Bill replied.

"How long you stay?" the man asked.

"One week," Bill said.

The man led us to our hut which was set back a short distance from the beach. We settled in, took a shower and then we decided to explore this tiny island before it got dark. We strolled around, looking at the seaside bar, the open-air restaurant and the white smooth sand lining the edge of the water.

"This place is gorgeous!" I held Bill's hand as we walked along the beach. It was like being in heaven.

"Pretty nice, huh?" Bill leaned against a palm tree, gazing out at the water. "You could put this view right onto a postcard, it is a tropical paradise. You want to come snorkelling with me tomorrow?" His eyes sparkled with anticipation. He couldn't wait to get out there.

"Absolutely!" I answered him as I walked up to the water's edge and paused as the sun began setting colouring the sky with a warm peach glow. As the sun slid from view behind the mountain, we walked along the sand and returned to our hut.

Bamboo Island, Thailand

Bill speaking with a soldier in front of our hut on Phi Phi Don Island

In the morning we walked back through the bush along the sandy path toward the main road. We met at the tourist shop along with three other couples who were going with us on the boat trip. There was a couple from Germany, another couple from Switzerland and a couple from France. Together we set out for the caves under the rising heat of the sun. On the way, the guide stopped the boat and told us that this would be a good spot for snorkelling. We all pulled on our fins and masks and dove into the water.

"Ohhhh! This is so refreshing, " I said. My mask had fogged up so I wiped it off and dove back under. The coral reefs were large, in colours of red and yellow. You could see where some of the reefs had been damaged by boat anchors. Chunks of coral were missing or were badly cracked. Fish swam by us, their colours bright and vivid in the clear water. I saw Bill in front of me looking at a brightly coloured fish with tall spikes along its head and back. He reached out to touch it and I tried to signal him not to do it. He didn't notice me and when his hand was about two inches away he suddenly hesitated. He held his arm steady not reaching any further. The fish looked like a dangerous one to me because it was so spiky and unusual looking. I gestured to Bill and we surfaced together.

"What kind of fish was that?" I asked him.

"I don't know. I saw a picture of one once before but I can't remember the name of it," he answered.

"Why didn't you touch it?"

"I don't know.......I wanted to but I think there's something about that fish.....maybe it's poisonous," he said.

"I tried to get your attention but you were too focused on that fish. Just be careful. There are lots of different sea creatures here that we know nothing about," I told him.

We climbed back into the boat with the others and lay back, asking each other questions about where we were from and what we did for a living. The couple from Switzerland spoke some English so we talked to them for awhile. They were travelling extensively through southern Asia and they had left Switzerland during a snow flurry.

"Well there's no snow here! Just beautiful beaches and beautiful water!" I smiled as I thought how cold it would be in Canada at this time of year.

We passed alongside exotic rock formations jutting up out of the water until we arrived at the caves. There were bamboo ladders leading upwards at impossibly steep angles. Everywhere there were bird droppings splattered against the sides of the cliffs. We were told that it was a very dangerous job for the men who climbed those ladders every day to collect the precious bird's nests. It was an interesting thing to see, and I wondered how many men would have fallen off those ladders to their deaths below. All that struggle for a dish enjoyed by a small group of people I thought.

As the day wore on and morning became afternoon, we planned to stop at Bamboo Beach before heading back to Phi-Phi Don. My skin had started turning red and I had several spots covering my body. It appeared that I had developed a bad heat rash and so I tried to keep my skin covered as much as possible.

As we pulled into Bamboo Beach we all held our breath as we gazed in silence at the view that lay before us. It was like a scene from a James Bond movie or a postcard. The sand was pure white, with bright blue water which was perfectly clear. The water was shallow and you see the ripples of the sand beneath. It was an uninhabited patch of land and there were virtually no other people around for miles, only jungle and wildlife. We sat on the beach and had our fresh seafood lunch. Bill took off down the beach to go exploring with the others. I badly wanted to get in the water and cool down but my skin was starting to blister and I had to remain sitting, hiding from the sun. As I sat on a small log, staring out at the water I noticed a movement in the water nearby. All I could see was something thin and black and it was moving rapidly across the top of the water.

"What the.........?" I stood up and as I took a step toward the water's edge I screamed and jumped backwards.

"It's a snake! Where are you guys? There is a SNAKE in the water!" I kept shouting until one of the couples swam towards me to see what all the noise was about.

I pointed frantically toward where the snake had been and I explained what I had seen. The couple could not speak much English but I think they understood and they got out of the water. I watched as the husband headed along the shore in the direction which the snake had gone. I sat back down with his wife and we waited for the guide to come back.

The guide walked over to us. "That is poisonous sea snake. We have poisonous sea snake in Thailand. Be careful, you see one do not go near, swim away fast as you can," he instructed.

We all looked at one another and I felt glad for the first time about having a horrible heat rash that had kept me out of the water. After a seven hour day out on the water, the guide brought us back to Phi-Phi Don Island. We were all exhausted but it had been a good day. Bill and I climbed straight into bed the moment we got back to our hut.

Later on, Bill and I sat on the deck of Charlie's Beach Bar beside the ocean, as we sipped our drinks and relaxed. A television had been set up with the cable running across the sand. It was tuned in to CNN. I sat staring at the newscaster, watching his lips move as the words rung through my ears. I froze in my seat, as I listened.

"...with the war in the Persian Gulf, it is thought that terrorists have been hiding out in Thailand. The Canadian and U.S. governments are warning citizens to avoid travelling in Thailand at this time...........". The broadcaster continued. "We have reason to believe that some of these terrorists, in an effort to blend in, are travelling as couples...... people are asked to be aware of any persons as described, and to report any suspicious behaviour to the authorities......".

Bill and I turned to look at each other and then at the others who were wordlessly sitting there with us, each one of us hanging on to every word.

"Bill, what does this mean?" I was nervous.

"Nothing yet. Don't worry about it. Let's just wait and see first," he said.

The next morning we woke up to find an armed soldier walking back and forth outside our hut, with a sub-machine gun strapped to his shoulder. We stepped outside and Bill went over to talk with him. I waited on the porch, not wanting to go near someone wearing a sub-machine gun whether they were friendly or not.

I watched as Bill spoke with him and then he wandered back over to me.

"He's actually here to protect us. He said many of the tourists have left the island and there may be terrorists trying to hide out in tourist areas to avoid being caught," Bill explained. He spoke as if he were talking about the weather, he seemed so calm.

"He....he said *what*?" I could feel myself start to shake.

"I'm sure we're absolutely safe here. He said that there were more than 100 armed soldiers posted on the island and they arrived last night," he said and shrugged.

"*One hundred* armed soldiers? Are you serious? On this little island?" I started pacing back and forth. Getting caught up in the Gulf War had not been part of my beach holiday plans. Even though we weren't in a combat zone, the thought of terrorists being among us didn't exactly make me feel safe. I could feel my anxiety escalate and so I decided to head straight for the beach to find some tourists to get some more information. As we walked along the beach we didn't spot one person, anywhere. We were completely alone.

"What, where are all the *people*?" I wondered aloud..

"I don't believe it. Everyone is gone." Bill said. He just stood there, looking up and down at the empty beach.

We continued walking, veering off the beach. We hiked through the bush and headed into the town. The island was all but deserted. We spoke to a local shop owner and we learned that the previous evening nearly every single tourist had left the island. How could that be? I shook my head in disbelief.

"Bill, how is it that several *hundred* people could have left and we had no idea?" I was in a state of bewilderment. "Why are *we* still here?"

Bill scratched his head as he looked at the ground. "Maybe we had too much to drink last night?" he asked.

"Oh, come on. That is not funny. This is really no time for jokes," I said.

It was like there had been a mass exodus all at once, only we, apparently, were in our own world and had no clue! All I kept thinking was that if there were over a hundred armed soldiers on an island without a single paved road and there was only us, how safe could it really be here? It was obvious to me that we stuck out like a sore thumb and we could, therefore, make an easy target for any terrorist wanting revenge on 'Americans' or western people. We walked back towards Charlie's Beach, not knowing what was going to happen, if anything. I started to calm down a little when Bill reminded me that these soldiers were here to protect us and because it seemed to be only us and over one hundred of them, we had a *lot* of protection. It was in the interest of the Thailand government to keep tourists safe and happy and I had to agree that made sense. I tried to push away my fears and we decided to head to the beach and try to relax for awhile.

As we sat on the beach that morning, I observed how different it was to see an empty beach. Without people around it was very quiet but also very scenic. About fifteen minutes after we had sat down on our bamboo mats, I was startled when I looked up and saw a Middle Eastern looking couple walking toward us. The beach was virtually empty but for some reason they chose to sit a few feet away from us. The fact that they would not look at us or acknowledge us in any way, yet they sat *right beside* us, raised red flags immediately. Their behaviour was stiff and they appeared very uncomfortable.

"This is beyond funny Bill. Do you see them? Why are they sitting beside us when the whole beach is empty?"

"They are probably tourists, like us," he answered. Bill agreed that it was a bit odd, but he seemed unconcerned.

"Hmmmm. Well, tell me then, why are they dressed in long pants and long sleeved shirts and not wearing shorts or bathing suits? They don't look like they're here for a swim or to enjoy a day at the beach if you know what I mean," I said. I couldn't keep the sarcasm out of my voice. "Doesn't it seem odd to you that *everyone* else has left, but they are still here?"

"Well, we are still here," Bill replied, with a laugh.

Bill kept looking out at the water. I asked myself if maybe I was overreacting. Maybe these two people were innocent tourists who happened to be as uninformed as we were or who didn't care. Maybe they didn't like getting tanned, maybe they were always this unfriendly..... My mind kept hearing the newscaster's words "be aware of any suspicious looking persons, travelling as couples....". I looked around me and noticed that several of the soldiers were standing close to the couple, observing them. I considered the facts: there were armed soldiers, an empty island, and news reports of terrorist activity in resort areas. It didn't seem like a good situation to me.

"Look Bill, you can either stay or come with me but I'm leaving, now." I instantly stood up, rolled up my bamboo mat and started walking toward our hut. I had decided to get out of here along with everyone else.

Bill stared after my retreating back. "You're not leaving! Sit down and don't be ridiculous. You're not going anywhere," he called out to me.

I stopped in my tracks, turned around and stared straight at him. "Watch me," I said.

I walked quickly back to our hut and started throwing my clothes into my bag. By the time Bill walked through the door I was ready to go.

"Kim, don't leave," he said. He looked upset.

"Where is everyone then Bill?" "Why the guns?" I demanded.

"Look, calm down. We'll find out what time the boat is leaving," he answered. Bill tried to be calm and reassuring.

"I'll tell you what time it's leaving. It's leaving now and I'm gonna be on it. Are you with me?" I stared expectantly at him.

Bill wearily packed up his things as I waited. He followed me out the door and together we hiked through the bush and onto the main road. I tried not to feel guilty as I knew he did not want to leave. But as I looked around and saw that the entire village was deserted I knew I was doing the right thing. There were no other tourists walking around laughing, swinging their backpacks or eating seafood in the restaurants. It was a ghost town. It was still and quiet except for our voices. I walked quickly down the road to the boat. It was leaving in twenty minutes. I sat on the beach and tried to stay clear headed.

"Goddamn it! Why do there always have to be wars? Why did Saddam Hussein have to ruin my vacation?" I was upset and angry at the same time.

Bill started to laugh and soon I was laughing with him. It was all so crazy. When the boat was ready to leave, we climbed on and stood at the bow, leaning on the railing as we pulled away. We were the only passengers. Sadly, we watched the peacefulness of Phi Phi Don slip away.

Back on Phuket Island, we rested in our bungalow in Kata Beach. Periodically, we would catch new reports coming out warning of terrorist cells operating in Thailand and I became increasingly agitated. I had never been remotely close to a war or terrorism and it was too close for comfort for me. I had a hard time coping with my fear for my safety. I had come here to *relax*, not worry about a war. We had

4 days left of our holiday but I felt like I couldn't last that long. The atmosphere here was now one of worry and tension. As we lay on the bed my eyes lost focus and I felt short of breath. There was a horrible tightening in my chest. Within moments my arms and legs began to go numb and tingly. I wondered if I was having a heart attack. I struggled to breathe but each time I inhaled I could only get in a little oxygen and my chest ached. I stood up but my legs gave out on me and I collapsed backwards onto the bed.

"Bill, I'm sorry...I have to get out of here. We have to leave. Something's happening....I don't know, my body......" I couldn't talk any more as I inhaled once again, getting very little air. I looked over at Bill, who was sitting on a chair staring at me. He seemed to understand that something was happening to me and it wasn't good. He stood up and grabbed our bags. He helped me walk outside to the patio where he sat me down while he checked out at the registration counter which was set up outside under a hut. He was busy talking to the man behind the counter while I tried to breathe, in, out, in, out. I had no feeling at all now in my arms and legs. By this time I felt close to unconsciousness.

"Can you call us a taxi please?" Bill asked for our passports to be returned and he came over and sat beside me.

A couple of minutes later a van pulled up and Bill helped me into the back. I lay back, trying to relax. We had been in the van about ten minutes when my breathing became very shallow and I started to breathe rapidly as I attempted to get air into my lungs. I looked down and was horrified to see my legs and arms twitching. I tried to speak but I couldn't. I looked at the driver for help and I noticed him observing me in his rear view mirror with a concerned look on his face.

"Take her to a doctor!" Bill's voice sounded far away.

"There is a hospital nearby. We are almost there," the driver responded. He glanced at me again as he pressed down hard on the gas pedal. Within five minutes we pulled up to the front of a small hospital where I was helped inside by Bill and the taxi driver. We entered an examination room. I could see a red cross sticker on the wall. My arms and legs were still shaking and my breathing was erratic.

"I don't know what's happening to her. She began doing this about half an hour ago," Bill explained to the doctor. I vaguely heard him answer some questions.

The doctor quietly filled a syringe with a golden coloured liquid and then came up to me.

"She'll be fine. Hyperventilation, it is very scary but she will soon be relaxed," he said to Bill. He then gently inserted the needle as I half-consciously wondered if it had been sterilized. Within seconds my arms and legs ceased twitching and I felt calm and sleepy. With enormous relief I realized that I could suddenly breathe again!

Moments later we were back in the taxi and the driver headed straight for the airport. Upon our arrival at the airport, an employee escorted me into a small dark room where I laid down on a cot so that I could rest. In the meantime, Bill waited nearby while the man took our airplane tickets to the airline officials who then rebooked our departure flight for our return to Japan. Within an hour we were put on the next flight to Japan.

As we settled into our seats, I squeezed Bill's hand.

"Thank you Bill, for helping me, " I said. I felt sad because he had really wanted to stay longer but it wasn't possible for me.

"No problem. It was better to get you out of there. We're going home now, and you'll be safe in Japan," he said reassuringly.

I was thinking how happy I had been less than two weeks earlier to leave Japan and head to a sunny destination for a holiday but now, as I sat in my plane seat, I was eager to get back to Osaka and my routine and predictable life.

Even though our holiday in Thailand was marred by the threat of terrorism, and by the media's relentless coverage of the war, I have never been treated more kindly or efficiently than by the people in Thailand. They were genuinely warm and caring people and I never forgot the gentle treatment I had received.

CHAPTER 10

A Farewell at Gonenbayashi

It was the middle of February as I sat hunched over the bathtub one morning, wringing out clothes. I hurriedly carried the dripping wet clothes out onto the balcony, trying to secure them on the clothesline while a biting cold wind blew up, sending some socks flying to the muddy ground below. I stood up, leaned over and stared at the dirty socks when the phone rang.

"Moshi moshi," I spoke into the phone.

"Keemoo. Hello, it is Yasko," she said. Her soft familiar voice was a welcome surprise.

"Hello Yasko! How have you been?"

"Just fine....thank you," she answered, letting out a small giggle.

"What are you doing this morning?" I asked her.

"I am doing my....how do you say....house chores? Just now I finish. Do you have free time?" she asked.

"Um, yeah, I just finished doing my laundry. Why don't we get together and go shopping?" I suggested.

"Ah, that is good idea. I must buy gift for my husband," she answered.

"I'll meet you in front of Kobeya Kitchen in an hour, is that okay?" I asked.

"In one hour. Okay. Good-bye Keemoo," Yasko said and hung up.

I replaced the phone and dashed into the bathroom. Two more shirts and a pair of pants still needed to be wrung out. For a moment I considered leaving them there in the tub but I knew with the cold wind outside that they would take forever to dry so I bent down and began squeezing the water out of the shirts. Within 30 minutes I was done and so I quickly put on some lipstick, ran a brush through my hair and I was out the door and on my way up the hill.

I had a few extra minutes so I decided to go into the pastry shop and buy some *kurikomon*. These were my favourite walnut pastries wrapped in a light dough and dusted with white icing sugar. They were expensive but delicious. I watched the lady delicately wrap my package with ribbons and wrapping paper. She placed my dessert into a fancy bag and handed it over the counter to me.

"Domo arigato!" I smiled as I walked back out to wait for Yasko.

She walked up in her white coat and black heels. I smiled as she approached but she looked different. Her face showed unhappiness. I thought it best if I let her mention anything on her own rather than push her. We took the train to Esaka to buy gifts for Valentine's Day. I had learned that in Japan, Valentine's Day was a day for men only and that meant the women would go out and buy chocolates and gifts for their boyfriends and husbands. To compensate for the women, a different day known as White Day followed soon after and the men would go out and buy gifts for the women. As we strolled through the aisles, fighting for space among the throngs of other shoppers, I was amazed at the variety of chocolates and love-themed gifts. Shopping in Japan was so over the top and I loved it!

"What do you buy for Bill?" Yasko asked me.

"Oh, I don't know. Probably white chocolate, that's his favourite. What will you get for your husband?"

"Some chocolate," Yasko said. She picked up a package of chocolate hearts and brought it over to the sales counter. I watched as the customer in front of us racked up US$70.00 for her chocolates. I would never have paid that much for chocolate at home in Canada but here it didn't seem inappropriate at all.

As we left the store, Yasko stopped walking for a moment.

"Keemoo. I must tell you something bad. I lost....a baby, last week. The doctor said I...must rest. He said....we can try for another baby in six months," she said quietly as she looked away.

I put my arm on her shoulder. "Yasko, I'm so sorry," I said. How do you heal a broken heart? I would have done anything in that moment to take away her pain. We fell silent for a moment, then we began walking again.

"Yasko, I must tell you something too," I said. She looked up at me, surprise in her face.

"Bill and I have decided to leave Japan sooner than we had planned. We will finish our classes in May and we are leaving on June 2," I said.

Yasko looked shocked for a moment. "Oh. I am sad to hear this. I will miss you. You have been good teacher...and good friend for me," she answered.

"But Keemoo, you must marry before you become Christmas cake!" Yasko admonished. I laughed at her remark. She was referencing a popular Japanese saying that if a woman didn't marry before her 25th birthday then she would become 'Christmas cake', a label not unlike that of old maid. As we walked together, I wondered what Yasko's life would be like when I was gone. She would have children, stay home and raise them. I would think of her, in her apartment, speaking English and cooking for her children. She was a very traditional Japanese woman, raised with strong values. But Yasko also had her own personality bubbling beneath the surface of social expectation. She was fragile on the outside but I knew she was a woman of strength on the inside. I was curious as to what she would have been had she had the opportunity to choose a career or a different life. My deepest hope for her was that she would be happy and that she would eventually have the child she wanted so much.

At the end of February we were expecting another visitor from home. Bill's brother Terry was coming to visit us. On the night of his arrival, Bill was teaching a late class near Kyoto and so it fell to me to meet Terry at the subway station. Bill was going to try to meet up with us as soon as he could. So I went to Umeda station so see if I could find Terry. It was late afternoon, rush hour, and the platforms were jam-packed with commuters heading home from work. I walked down to one platform and scanned the walls, looking for him. I couldn't see him so I went to the other side and hoped he might be waiting on another platform. I looked at my watch. It was 6:30 p.m. Where was he? I began to think that he had been given the wrong directions, or more likely, he was lost. I rounded the stairs yet again and as I walked down I could see Terry sitting on a bench halfway down the platform. I waved my arms as I worked my way through the mass of people to get over to him.

"Terry! How are you?"

"Good!" We gave each other a hug and I sat down beside him as we waited for Bill to meet up with us.

"Bill's on his way. He shouldn't be too long. Were you lost? How long have you been waiting here?"

"About an hour. I looked around but I couldn't see you. It's pretty crowded here," he said.

"Welcome to Japan. It's also rush hour right now and everyone is heading home so it's always crazy at this time of day. How's the shop doing?"

"It's pretty busy. I needed a vacation," he answered.

I could see Terry was exhausted and I hoped Bill wouldn't be much longer. Terry looked like he could use a rest. We waited about 15 minutes when I saw Bill come running down the stairs toward us.

"Hi Ter! Good to see you. How was the flight?"

"A long one. Good to see you too," he said as they gave each other a quick hug.

We stood up and squeezed in behind the people waiting for the train. When the train came down the tracks and the doors slid open we all herded in, one large mass of people. I stood by the window, trying to avoid being pinched or touched as often happened, and I listened to Bill and Terry catch each other up on their lives. Bill was eager to show Terry our little place.

"We live not too far from here. It's a real nice neighbourhood. Our apartment is pretty tiny but it's new and nice," he explained.

I pressed my nose against the glass, feeling tired myself. I had been teaching all day and my feet were sore from standing and walking all day. Tomorrow was going to be even busier. I had classes to teach and we wanted to show Terry around Osaka as well. I closed my eyes and listened to the monotonous voice coming from the speakers "Ryokuchi-koen des! Ryokuchi-koen des!" as it announced our stop.

When we finally made it back to the apartment we gave Terry a quick tour and he seemed surprised that we were living in such a small space. There wasn't much to show him.

"Here's the kitchen, where we hang out. There's our room and here's your room which we use for teaching private students. The space became even smaller when there were three people sharing it together. We explained to Terry that Japanese people live in much smaller homes than we were accustomed to in North America.

The next few days were a whirlwind of sightseeing. Bill and I took Terry to the Kyamizu-Dera Temple in Kyoto, the castle in Osaka, and we also went to Shika-koen, the deer park in nearby Nara City. The temple we visited in Nara City was one of our favourites and Bill and I had been there several times before. It was higher up in the mountains and so the weather was bitterly cold. We all had our ski coats on but still it was a challenge to keep warm. We stopped and bought deer biscuits which we then fed to the deer. After seeing the temple we stopped in at a local restaurant for lunch. We all had noodle soup to warm up. It was fun to be around family again and to speak English with someone other than our students.

After a couple of days Terry decided to head down to Hiroshima on the Shinkansen bullet train. He was going to go on his own and so we gave him train maps and accompanied him to Umeda station where he boarded the bullet train.

"Have a good time!" We both shouted out to him and he waved back as he walked down the platform.

It had been so nice to see a familiar face again and I started to think ahead to the summer when we would be going home. Even though I was excited at the idea of returning home to Canada after almost two years away, I still had mixed feelings. Japan had become our home and we were comfortable with our jobs and our lifestyle. We had made friends and places were familiar now. I thought about how hard it had been for us in the beginning and how we would be walking away from all that we had achieved. We would have to start all over again when we returned to Canada. There were also many things that had to be done before we left Japan. We would have to start lining up replacement teachers for our private students, arrange to give away our furniture and we needed to organize our travel plans.

I wrote a letter to my parents in L.A. to make arrangements to visit them on our way home. We were also planning on stopping over in Hawaii for a week to relax. I looked around at the apartment wistfully. We had accumulated so many things, paintings I had done, gifts we had received, new cushions I had bought for our chairs, ceramic pottery from Laura...... I would miss our little apartment.

Terry returned from his tour of Hiroshima and southern Honshu three days later. He told us about the museum that had been established in memory of the victims of the atomic bomb. He had done a lot of walking and touring around the city. It had been an interesting trip for him and he looked more rested than when he had arrived.

The following day we walked to the train station to see Terry off. I could see that Bill was upset and that he was going to miss his brother. After Terry bought his ticket, we waved good-bye and stood watching as he disappeared down the subway stairs.

"See you in a few months!" Bill called after him. Then a second later Terry was gone from sight.

Not long after Terry left, Bill and I decided to travel to Kyoto for a weekend of sightseeing. We wanted to do some shopping and visit the Golden Temple once again. It was still early in the year and the weather hadn't warmed up yet but we thought it would be a great trip nonetheless to revisit some of the places we had seen when we had first visited the city.

After taking the train to Kyoto, we headed to a ryokan where we dropped off our weekend bags. Again we were struck by the tranquillity of Kyoto, with the ever present mountains cradling the city. On Saturday morning, Bill and I had a light breakfast and walked to the station that would take us to the Golden Temple. Along the way, we saw several geishas walking in the streets, their magnificent kimonos wrapped snugly around their bodies. I wondered how they managed to move so efficiently while wearing thick white socks and wooden platform shoes. I noticed all of the decorative details such as their hair combs and fans. There were little signs of the modern day influence though with the sight of their umbrellas and purses slung over their arms..We walked through the rain, admiring the quaint little shops lining the road side. There was a sweet and fresh smell in the air of Kyoto, and it was a much quieter city than Osaka.

Bill at the Golden Temple

Me at the Golden Temple

It was a short journey to the temple and at this time of year it wasn't too crowded as the cherry blossom trees were not in bloom and the vegetation was still under winter's grip. Walking around the pond, we stopped to feed the fish and enjoy the beauty of the temple. I thought about how much we had experienced since we first gazed upon this temple the previous year and how much we had learned along the way. There was a joy to our lives now as we had finally begun to assimilate to the culture and of course we were now earning a good living as well. Bill and I took a photo of each other standing by the pond with the temple in the background. We thought about how nice it would be to visit the temple during each season of the year and compare the scenery. Our weekend trip to Kyoto was over before we knew it and it was time to head back home and prepare for another work week ahead.

~

Soon winter gave way to spring. The early months of spring had been warm and clear. As April turned into May, the skies became bluer and the cherry blossoms bloomed and died once again, signalling another passing season. I was on my way this Sunday afternoon for my final lesson with Momoyo and her grandson. I hadn't seen her for awhile as she frequently cancelled classes because she often didn't feel well. When I arrived at her apartment for the last time, I was invited in and I sat at the dining room table where her grandson was busy studying his kanji characters. I had brought a children's book with me and I showed it to him. He was interested in the pictures. I let him flip through the pages, pausing occasionally to sound out words for him. He suddenly pointed at a picture of the sun on one of the pages and he began talking animatedly with his grandmother. Momoyo listened patiently then said something to him which seemed to appease him. I looked at her expectantly.

"My grandson said that the sun is not yellow like in your book. It is red," she said.

I held the book up and pointed out the sun to her. "But it *is* yellow. Look at the picture," I said to her. I didn't understand what she was trying to say. I thought she was confusing the different words for the colours.

"No. In Japan the sun is not yellow. It is red. That is what we see and that is what is on our flag," she explained.

I sat still for a moment, absorbing this information, trying to understand. All my life since childhood I had been taught that the sun was yellow and that is how we coloured it and that is how it appeared in the sky. I suddenly realized that Momoyo and her grandson were right. The sun was indeed red in appearance in Japan and that is how the Japanese people saw it. I understood that even though my perception was different from people in Japan, we were both essentially right. It was a difference in culture and in reality, for at night the sun here was a brilliant red. In that moment, my whole experience of living in Japan came into focus as I appreciated the fact that it was okay to be different as long as we respected each other's differences. I was amazed that a simple remark from a young child could bring about such profound clarity. I shook my head in wonder as I continued reading the book to him. He became bored after a couple of minutes and so I took out another book and began my lesson with Momoyo.

At the end of our lesson, her entire family arrived to share coffee and cake and to say good-bye. It was an emotional evening as I knew I would never see this family again and yet they had been so kind to me and I had gained so much from my interactions and afternoons spent with them. I hugged Momoyo warmly as I left, hoping that her health would improve and that she would spend her last years in happiness with her children and grandchildren.

One afternoon in the middle of May, Bill and I were heading to the school to hand in our textbooks and finish up our student attendance sheets. We got off the train at Shinsaibashi station. As we walked through the shopping district Bill suddenly stopped.

"Hey look! It's the Batman car!" He pointed to a long, winged, black car that was parked at an angle on the sidewalk. Several people were milling around it, taking photos.

"Is that the real one, from the movie?" I asked him.

"I think so. Let's go take a look," he said.

We wandered over and read the sign posted beside the car. Judging by the reactions of the onlookers, it was indeed the actual Batman car. Japanese people were known for paying exorbitant prices for advertising and entertainment. We laughed and wondered how much it would have cost to ship that car all the way here and keep it on display. As we threaded our way through hordes of people we heard murmurs of "gaijin" repeatedly. But we were now immune to the stares and comments that were made in our presence. We had been here almost two years and I am sure that we were recognizable to several people in various neighbourhoods that we frequently passed through.

We finished our work at the school and Masa explained to us that we would not be receiving our yearly bonuses because we were ending our contract early. He had tried to encourage us to stay until August so that we could receive our bonuses but our minds were set on returning home. We placed the text books on the shelf and spent a bit of time talking to staff and teachers. There were many of us leaving this year and it was bittersweet to say good-bye to people who had shared this experience alongside us.

After leaving the school, we decided to go see a movie in Umeda. Interestingly, going to a movie in Japan is listed in guidebooks as one of the seven dangers in Japan, others being earthquakes and typhoons. The reason for this is that when the large number of people rush in to find a seat, occasionally a person is crushed to death. We had recently seen Pretty Woman and Sleeping with the Enemy and today we were going to see Dances with Wolves. For Bill and I it was like having the upper hand whenever we went to see a movie because the movies were in English with Japanese subtitles and so we could pick up on the nuances and idioms that were mainly lost on the Japanese audiences. As we sat there watching Kevin Costner, feeling like lottery winners for having seats, Bill suddenly let out a loud husky laugh. His laugh echoed through the entire theatre and cut through the silence like a knife. Literally every head turned in unison in our direction. I shrank back in my seat in embarrassment but Bill kept on laughing at the joke on the screen.

"Yes, Bill, that was funny but do you have to be so...*loud*?"

That just made him laugh even harder. At the end of the movie I had to literally hang on to Bill's arm as he pushed his way through people to get to the exit. At one point I got slammed into the wall right near the door and another woman nearby began yelling in panic as she too got hemmed in and shoved up against the wall. Bill instantly swung his body around and freed us both, using his size and strength to propel us forward and out the door. Wow, they weren't kidding about this being dangerous, I thought to myself.

Though we saw the movie again two years later, we never forgot that day we had sat watching it in Umeda. That experience was more moving and entertaining by far, as we drank it in, hanging on to the familiarity of our native language and the luxury at being able to understand what was being said.

The weather gradually became warmer and we could feel a familiar trace of the wetness in the air coming. Towards the end of May we sold our bikes, gave away our furniture and shipped some boxes of clothing and gifts home to Canada. We had learned the hard way how to travel more lightly, although we were still taking six suitcases back with us.

Finally, our last night in the apartment arrived. I remembered how happy I had been when we got settled in and had our own place. I looked around the rooms. The only sign that we had been here were the tiny marks in the window frame in the kitchen where I had pinned airmail paper up for privacy. We curled up together in our futon and talked late into the night.

In the morning, we threw our last things into our suitcases and bundled up our futons which we were going to leave on the sidewalk. I folded up the *yukata* that I had bought in Kyoto and I carefully placed it in my duffel bag. Everything was done. It was time to go. I looked out the little kitchen window, now bare of its paper covering, and I stared at the elementary school across the street. How many times had I watched the children from the balcony, as they did their morning exercises in the schoolyard? Many, I thought to myself. I looked up and down the street and remembered the man in the car who had followed me home one night. I tried to imprint all these memories, and the buildings, signposts and drink machines into my brain so that I would always have a memory of my life here. After making sure the apartment was clean, we shut the door behind us for the last time.

We walked down the steps and I glanced back once, thinking how we would no longer receive mail in our mail slot, or have friends or students ringing our doorbell. We waited at the bottom of the stairs for Mali, one of my private students, who was going to escort us to a nearby hotel where we would stay for a couple of nights until we left. Later on in the evening, we were going to a farewell party held in our honour at Gonenbayashi restaurant in Esaka. Some of the teachers from Interac and some of the staff would be there to say goodbye to us.

Gonenbayashi was very crowded. It was the first of the month again. We saw our party in one of the side rooms and we headed straight over. I had butterflies in my stomach as I was excited to be returning home but I was also sad about leaving my life behind here, especially the people we knew.

"Hey, Bill, Kim!" Masa and Taeko shouted out to us as we took a seat at the table.

"Pass the chu-hai!" I laughed as I reached out for a drink on the table.

"Drink up you guys!" B.J. raised his arm in a toast. "To your last night in Japan! Kanpai!"

We all raised our glasses and chugged down the sake and mango juice. As we sat together, we reminisced about our various classes and sight-seeing excursions, the challenges of being a foreigner in Japan, the good times we had all had and, of course, the daily reality of the trains. I noticed that there were new faces around the table which was an inevitable reality as teachers working overseas constantly came and went. Lisa and Barbara had left a month before us and they were trav-elling through Thailand before heading home to the United States. It seemed that a lot of us were leaving this summer. Now it was our turn and I had mixed feelings. I realized that I would likely never see these people again, people who we had grown close to and shared some life changing adventures with. I picked at the rice in front me and then I wiped my face with a hot towel to hide the tears that I knew were com-ing. Now that our time to leave was finally here, I didn't want to go yet.

We drank and partied until midnight. Some of our private students had shown up and it was a warm and emotional farewell. The night ended with pictures being taken and students crying at our depar-ture. As Bill and I got up to leave, we hugged everyone one last time.

We glanced back, trying to remember each one of their faces. "Good-bye you guys!" they all shouted out in unison.

I turned around and with a heavy heart walked up the stairs to the street above. We walked to the hotel in the dark, by now familiar with many of the side roads and buildings. We were staying at a business hotel which was really nothing more than a closet sized room just wide enough to walk in. You had to get into the bed from the direction you walked in as there was no room to turn around. Our suitcases were piled up, obscuring the window. We slept soundly, jolted awake by the alarm clock at 7:00 the next morning. We showered and dressed and then left our luggage in the lobby. We had three hours to ourselves before heading to the airport.

Bill and I walked over to Higashi-Mikuni station and took the train to Umeda. Since we had so much time we decided to go one last time to Big Man book store which was a well-known book store where many foreigners were able to get books in English. There were hundreds of English books and magazines and I had spent many afternoons there killing time between classes. On occasion, we would run into familiar faces while browsing the books and it was a great opportunity to share gossip and information and keep each other informed. Today, there was no one at the store whom we knew but we browsed anyway. As we looked at the texts used for teaching English, we realized that we would probably never have the opportunity to use them again. After awhile our stomachs were growling and we thought it would be a good idea to have a nice meal before going to the airport. Along the way, we passed a pachinko parlour that Bill had taken his brother Terry to a few months earlier. We wandered along the streets, looking at everything one last time. We saw all the white cars zooming by on the expressway above. We picked up our luggage at the hotel and then walked down the street to the subway. We came across a little Italian restaurant that we hadn't known was there and it looked nice so we went in had our lunch. The food was incredibly good and we smiled to each other, wishing we had found this place earlier. After finishing our lunch, it was time to go so we headed over to the subway and took the train to the airport.

Leaving Japan, Osaka International Airport June 1991

It was early afternoon when Bill and I arrived at Osaka International Airport and checked in our luggage. We proceeded through customs to turn in our alien registration cards. I fished through my purse and found mine as I pestered Bill to hurry up and find his. I quickly passed through customs and while I was waiting for Bill to follow me I stepped over to a little kiosk which sold duty free cosmetics. I browsed the perfumes and make-up for a few minutes and then I turned around to look for Bill. He was nowhere in sight. Where the heck was he?

I started to panic when I couldn't find him. He had literally disappeared from sight. There was no way he could have passed me and gone down the hall so I traced my steps back to see if he was still in customs. Our plane was due to leave in twenty minutes and I felt my anxiety rise when I couldn't find him anywhere. It was then that

I just happened to notice the top of his head from the window of an office at the side of the customs area. Oh God. What could possibly be wrong? I didn't hesitate for a second. I ran over and literally raced right through customs past several customs officers who were waving and yelling at me to stop. I ignored them and barged straight into the office where a startled customs officer looked up while Bill sat in a chair, his face displaying no emotion. The man who was seated looked very angry as he glared at me while the other man standing behind Bill reached over to grab me.

"It's alright. She's my fiancé," Bill said. He looked scared.

"What's going on? What's the problem? We have a plane to catch!" I said in alarm. I looked at both men, expecting an answer. They did not respond.

Bill looked over at me. "I lost my alien registration card. They think it's in my luggage and they are taking it off the plane to look for it. I tried to tell them that it's not in my luggage, that I lost it. I don't think they understand," he told me. He looked away for a moment. "Actually, I threw it away a couple of days ago, I didn't think I needed it anymore," he added.

"Bill, how could you do this? You *need* that card to get out of the country. You don't just throw away official documents!" I was incredulous. "We're going to miss our plane!" The old familiar panic started to well up inside of me as I envisioned myself being led away with Bill into police custody. I could not get over the fact that Bill would show such poor judgment.

The man sitting at the desk did not look up at either of us. He was busy writing something down and making phone calls.

"We can't find your registration card. Where is it?" he asked in a serious voice.

Didn't he just hear what Bill had told me? It was gone, thrown out, I wanted to scream at him.

Bill continued to sit calmly as he tried to answer the official once more. "I told you it's gone. I threw it away. I didn't think I needed it anymore," he answered.

There was another call made as we waited anxiously. I looked at my watch. We had ten minutes until departure time. *Ten minutes.*

The man at the desk spoke up again. "Are you planning on returning to Japan?" he asked Bill.

"No." Bill replied flatly.

"In that case, you can sign this paper here. Ordinarily you cannot leave Japan without one," he said. His tone was matter of fact.

"Show me where to sign," Bill said. He was given a pen and he quickly wrote his signature on the form. Once this was done, we were allowed to leave, but we were told it would be done under escort. We had 7 minutes to make it to the gate. We ran as fast as we could behind the escort, our hearts pounding. Breathless, we made it to the final security checkpoint where I was asked to put my purse on the table for a routine search. I continued glancing at my watch, worried we would never make our flight. Suddenly, the young woman going through my purse held up a large pair of scissors and began talking sternly to me.

"What is this?" she demanded. "You have weapon!" she held the scissors up for everyone to see.

"No, no, those are my hair cutting scissors!" I gestured with my fingers as though I were cutting my hair. How could I explain to her that in Japan it had been a nightmare trying to find a salon willing to work with me? Stylists were unwilling to colour, trim or style my hair and I was told over and over that my hair was different from Japanese hair. I was told that Japanese hair is very coarse and even cutting my hair was something stylists were not interested in doing. Because of this and the language barrier, I had purchased these scissors to trim my own hair.

"You cannot take weapon on airplane!" the woman yelled at me.

By now my heart rate was off the charts yet I tried to remain calm. My goal was getting on that plane.

"Look, those are salon scissors. See? Look at the serrated edges. I have no interest in them now, so you can keep them, okay?" I smiled up at her.

The woman hesitated only for a second and then very abruptly she pointed us toward the boarding gate. Bill and I followed our escort through the door, down the ramp and onto the plane where the flight attendant was waiting for us. She led us to our seats and as I sat down I was an emotional wreck. I felt tremendous relief that we had made the flight.

After the plane took off, the flight attendant handed out steaming hot towels for our faces and hands and we both sat back, reflecting on how close we had come to missing the plane. All at once the stress vanished and Bill and I laughed hysterically at the craziness of our situation. We had experienced so many life changing moments while living in Japan and even our departure was another dramatic story in itself.

"How many hours till we get to Hawaii?" I asked him.

"Seven, eight? I don't know, I only know that I'm glad we're on our way," he said. He gave me a smile and his eyes shone with amusement.

"Yes, Hawaii. Not the Aleutian Islands this time," I said softly as I stretched out my legs and looked out the window at the clouds below. I looked forward to sunshine and warm water and time to relax and unwind before returning home.

Upon our return to Canada, we found ourselves in yet another ambiguous state of being. While it was wonderful to be home, it involved, nonetheless, many months of adapting to being surrounded by western customs, less crowds, eating with forks, and laying in a bathtub that was longer than our bodies. It was a time of reverse culture shock. It took Bill many months to stop bowing to people in public and for me to stop standing at elevators, looking like a fool while the men wondered what I was doing while I was waiting for them to go in first. I also found that we were always well dressed where most people in Vancouver dressed very casually. We had to get used to driving a car again and hearing English every day which was almost overwhelming at first. Once again, we were faced with the daunting task of finding jobs, a place to live, and transportation. These and many other changes would take us a long time to adjust to. Japan had altered our life and given us an incredible experience. I was grateful for it and I wouldn't change it. I had developed an emotional connection to the country now and many of its customs. I would miss the people, the job we had, the delicate scent of peaches in the air during autumn, the gorgeous temples and the many delicious treats we had come to love. But most of all, I would remember that we had arrived with nothing and yet we had carved out an existence through sheer determination and hard work and it had provided us with an experience that comes once in a lifetime.

ACKNOWLEDGMENTS

I want to thank my family for their unending support of my endeavour to write this story. They have accompanied me on this journey from the very beginning and their suggestions and comments were heartfelt. Their opinions were valued and they encouraged me through the endless writing and re-writing.

I also wish to thank my colleague, Teresa Morishita, a faculty member at Kwantlen Polytechnic University, for her helpful and uncanny feedback and for the time she took to read my manuscript. As a fellow gaijin, her insights were much appreciated.

Thanks are due to the many friends I made while living in Japan. During some of the most challenging moments I was shown compassion and friendship in a foreign land. I will never forget them. Without these relationships, I would not have had a story to write.

Thank you also to Nancy Lee Parish, a fellow author, who inspired me to bring my story to print.

I am also grateful to my cousin Bonnie Scott, without whom this project would not have been finished. Sometimes it takes an artist to motivate another.

20304936R00104

Made in the USA
Charleston, SC
05 July 2013